TEACHING AGILITY
A manual for instructors and handlers

Peter Lewis and John Gilbert

Illustrations:
Peter Lewis

Photographs:
Marc Henrie

Front cover photograph:
Anthony Reynolds LBIPP, LMPA

Front cover:
The authors discussing course building at the
Pedigree Chum 1993 Agility Stakes finals,
Olympia, London.

CANINE PUBLICATIONS

21 Burridge Road, Burridge, Southampton, SO3 7BY
Telephone 0489 885112

TEACHING AGILITY
A manual for instructors and handlers

First published 1994

ISBN 0 906422 10 8

Printed and bound in Great Britain by
BPCC Wheatons Ltd
Typeset by Canine Publications in Times New Roman 10/11

Contents

5. *The Basis of Free Style Handling*
   Working with three hurdles - Recall jumping -
   Working on - Working on with control - Changing sides -
   Choosing handling sides - Directional control from behind -
   Continuing after recall jumping

6. *Final Handling Preparation and Sequences.*
   Commands & hand signals - Body language -
   Working every obstacle - Sequences -
   Full course sequences -

7. *The Competition Class.*
   Dividing handlers by standard & saving time -
   Building the right courses -
   Running courses without jumping -
   Weaving improvement - Critiques of Complete Rounds

8. *Agility Problems:-*
   Fitness & safety - The dog - General control - Praise -
   The use of toys - The use of tit-bits -
   General handling mistakes -
   Bad habits - Speed - The start - Hurdle type obstacles - Table -
   Tunnels - Hoop or tyre - Long jump - Contact equipment -
   Weaving poles

COLOUR ILLUSTRATIONS

ILLUSTRATIONS

In the text

Introducing the Manual

We have both had a long love affair with dog training and when Agility came along it was a natural progression to become involved with what promised to be a fascinating sport. It was through Agility that we became friends and quickly came to recognise that we had similar ideas about the direction of the sport. We were instructing Agility at our own clubs and as guests for others and it was not long before we took our first seminar together. It was about Agility judging, a subject that required much attention during the early days and still does. Next we were asked to take Instructors Seminars which we have done on many occasions since. We put to good use our combined dog behaviour and training knowledge which has spanned in excess of 56 years. Allied to this was what we had learned about Agility thus far. This then became the basis of the Agility Instructors Seminars that we have conducted since. We have had enormous pleasure teaching others knowing that they would in turn be passing their knowledge on and we in turn are still learning. We have a never ending search for the perfect method of teaching any facet of the Sport and this manual is the result of our endeavours so far.

The manual is aimed at existing instructors or those who are about to take on what should be an exacting task. It is also of great benefit for handlers who want to understand how they can improve their dog and increase their all round Agility training knowledge.

In our opinion it is not necessary for Agility instructors to currently be prolific winners of competition prizes, nor is it entirely necessary for them to have been regular prize winners in the past. Indeed just as some top handlers make poor judges this anomaly can be true as far as instructors are concerned.

Some winners are not that aware how they have achieved good results but their club instructor should be. Far better that the instructor is a student of good practice, although it is necessary for considerable Agility handling to have been undertaken at least in the past. Unfortunately it is a fact of life that an instructor who has acquired a reputation as a good competition handler, either currently or in the past, is more likely to quickly gain the respect of his competition pupils. Conversely it is also possible to establish one's own reputation as an instructor without great previous handling success.

While most instructors are able to help new handlers to get their dogs to negotiate Agility obstacles, often they lack the logical step by step approach. When it comes to teaching handlers who are already competing with one or more dogs very often instruction is non existent. Maybe this is for a variety of reasons but usually not the least because competition handlers often win more prizes than their instructor who is loathe to criticise. To be fair this has always been a curse of the dog training world and not just Agility. Instructors often lack confidence to try and help successful handlers but it must be remembered that everyone needs a coach. It is not possible for us to see ourselves as others see us. Not only does this hold good in life generally but definitely as dog handlers as it is easier for others to watch our handling and to advise improvements. For instance incorrect timing of commands or unwittingly transmitting messages to our dog by poor body language are better observed as an overall picture. A good instructor will be able to give a far better assessment of dog and handler partnership than the handler alone.

All the methods explained herein are designed to produce free style Agility handlers. If your desire is to teach Agility handlers to run their dogs around at heel then this manual is not for you.

Free style Agility handling is the ability to work a dog irrespective of his relation to his handler's position. It may be that the dog is to be recalled from a start or pause, to work forward or on either side of the handler. To handle in this manner requires a degree of control that can only be described as instantaneous. Bring all such factors together and you have a freestyler. Watching this style of handling at a high level is literally poetry in motion for the Agility enthusiast. If that dog is also obviously happy doing what he is asked then we have something which has to be a good advertisement for dogs.

If any of your pupils tell you that they wish to try Agility because they are not very good at other dog disciplines then you have some work to do. The sport demands some very special attributes of dog handling that are not required in other training programmes but at the top it additionally requires an ability to gain instant response to commands and signals from a dog travelling at speed. Agility does look quite easy but without doubt it is a combination of speed and control that wins prizes. It is not that difficult to obtain a clear round on a tricky course with a slow reasonably obedient dog. What is difficult is handling and directing a fast dog. There is no substitute for instantaneous control mainly applied between the obstacles for this is where Agility prizes are won.

Obviously our aim has been to produce a manual that will enable handlers to take their dogs all the way to the top. We are, however, mindful of the fact that there are many people who have no such aspirations, preferring to participate in the sport just for fun. Contrary to popular opinion not everybody either expects or feels the necessity of striving to beat all comers. Maybe a clear round, albeit at a more comfortable pace than others, will be sufficient reward for some while just taking part satisfies others. All should be welcome and given equal attention when teaching.

A manual will often tell readers how to build or construct something so that they can make the maximum use of their investment. It may be a project that they have undertaken or just a question of getting the best performance from a purchase. Dogs are also an investment but usually in happiness. Just owning and enjoying them is sufficient happiness for millions. Others want to do something more with their dogs such as give them an activity. This in turn gives the owners even more happiness when their dogs are cleverly working for them. The pages of this manual will guide instructors along a logical path with the aim of achieving happy clever dogs and handlers as a final result.

All aspects of Agility instruction are covered. In the first place the manual explains teaching psychology. It sets out to give instructors a clear step by step approach to basic obstacle instructing. It gives valuable advice on teaching pupils how to put together sequences of obstacles and progressing towards course handling.

Competition handlers sometimes think they do not need help but invariably they do. Explanations of what to look for so that improvements can be suggested is explained. Then there is the handler who has an Agility problem. In many cases they can be told that the problem is a result of poor initial handling but that is cold comfort to someone desperate for a cure. Looking for remedies without establishing the cause can often be to treat the symptom but ignore the cause. Establishing a probable cause will often lead to a logical remedy. This manual endeavours to arm instructors with knowledge as to why any problem should have occurred in the first place so that choosing the best cure from alternatives becomes easier. Any remedial suggestions for dog behaviour is best tackled in this manner.

In short it is exactly what it says, an Agility Instructors Manual. Not only will instructors benefit from its advice but its pages should considerably extend any dog trainers knowledge of Agility and dog training in general. The manual will help to ensure that an instructor is equipped with sufficient knowledge to confidently take a class or improve an individual's handling techniques. Always remember that an Agility instructor should be just that, an instructor and not just a steward. It takes no skill to tell someone their dog missed a contact or knocked a pole down but it takes an instructor to give advice on why it occurred and how to avoid such problems in the future.

1

The Agility Instructor and Teaching Psychology

Most Agility instructors commence this facet of the sport at club level. However it is not sufficient just to be willing to take a class or wish to seem important. A desire to help others should over-ride the two previous possible considerations, but many other factors should also be considered. Not least is some understanding about how people learn and, apart from qualifications to be an instructor, this chapter should help potential instructors to have the right approach to their task.

THE ATTRIBUTES OF AN AGILITY INSTRUCTOR

1. Have a comprehensive knowledge of the sport and its rules.

An instructor must be the fountain of all Agility knowledge. Obviously all beginner Agility handlers will need just the simplest explanations of the rules, whereas many competition handlers are unsure of rules in detail. Agility rules must therefore be fully understood so that erroneous information is not passed on.

2. Have had considerable Agility handling experience.

To be an instructor of Agility without handling experience leaves an instructor without the feel for certain handling problems. When a handler makes a mistake it is easier to give advice if the instructor has made the same mistake in the past. Agility handling experience with dogs of different natures is also beneficial. There is no substitute for vast hands on experience when teaching dog training.

3. Have patience and understanding of people.

This is dealt with in greater detail under the heading of teaching psychology. The statement sounds logical but there is an art in putting your subject over even though you have vast Agility training knowledge.

4. Have a positive approach to problem solving.

When someone has a problem tackle it in a logical manner. Try to ascertain the cause of the problem first and then give advice. Understanding the cause will often produce a logical remedy or help you work your way towards one.

5. Know as many methods as possible of teaching.

Not all dogs are the same neither do they have the same reactions in certain situations. In this respect they are not unlike humans. Apart from your tried and trusted method it is therefore necessary to have in depth knowledge of alternative methods.

6. Be able to assess the ability of dog and handler quickly.

In many ways your experience under heading number 2 as an Agility handler will help you make a quick accurate assessment. The handling ability of both dog and handler may be quickly determined but the temperament of the handler may not. In this case refer to teaching psychology.

7. Always bear in mind the dog's safety.

The dog and his safety has to be your main consideration. In the first place for the dog's sake and also for the good name of the sport. Ensure the obstacles have no dangerous protrusions and can be considered safe. Do not allow handlers to do anything which will put the dogs safety and well being at risk in any way.

8. Not allow inexperienced handlers to work without supervision.

Ensuring that you know what the inexperienced are doing will help to ensure the dogs safety. Handlers may have misunderstood your requirements or they may think they know better than you. Their unsupervised actions may be cruel or unsafe or they may have a deleterious effect on the dogs training progress.

9. Be aware of the different traits of breed that may be encountered.

In the U.K. Collies dominate the sport. In many other countries they do not. A good instructor must understand the different traits of breeds of dog and understand the limitations of some.

10. Know when pupils should stop working their dog.

Some people never know when to stop and without supervision will go on and on training. Good instructors will stop them training when they feel that continuation is not in the dog's best interest.

11. Have ability to teach their subject in a pleasant manner.

Not just a case of good manners but more a question of making the subject interesting. Again refer to teaching psychology for greater detail.

12. Instruct and never just steward.

It is not that difficult to impress new pupils with your knowledge for, even though it may unfortunately be very limited, you will still know more than them. In other words you can get away with it. With competition handlers this becomes more difficult and in many cases competition classes are not instructed. This manual addresses this problem but A GOOD INSTRUCTOR INSTRUCTS AND DOES NOT STEWARD.

Summary:-

An Agility instructor should:-

1. Have a comprehensive knowledge of the sport and its rules.
2. Have had considerable Agility handling experience.
3. Have patience and understanding of people.
4. Have a positive approach to problem solving.
5. Know as many methods as possible of teaching.
6. Be able to assess the ability of dog and handler quickly.
7. Always bear in mind the dog's safety.
8. Not allow inexperienced handlers to work without supervision.
9. Be aware of the different traits of breeds that may be encountered.
10. Know when pupils should stop working their dog.
11. Have ability to teach their subject in a pleasant manner.
12. Instruct and never just steward.

★　★　★

TEACHING PSYCHOLOGY APPLIED TO AGILITY

STARTING TO TEACH

1. To be a good instructor one must first be a pupil. Analyse others teaching techniques to improve on them where possible.
2. Remember that people only learn if they want to so make it interesting.

PREPARATION

1. Thorough planning of the class to be taken is essential.
2. Keep notes or records of the dogs and handlers progress to help your planning.
3. Ensure prior preparation of equipment and training aids.
4. If you have a lot of new pupils then label everyone with at least their first name and the name of their dog.
5. Know your subject revise if necessary, you must exude confidence.
6. Prepare to speak with style and demonstrate with skill.
7. Develop the art of listening.

ATTENTION

1. Modulate the tone of voice.
2. Use a statement that excites attention or arouses curiosity.
3. Use analogies to convince pupils about your methods.
4. Ask a challenging question.
5. Tell a humorous story that relates to dog training.
6. Look into people's eyes, don't avoid them.
7. State facts to illustrate your point.
8. Use phrases or repeat words to indelibly stamp the memory.
9. Ask questions to keep pupils awake.

CLASSES

1. Remember if you want pupils to come back not only must you teach but also entertain.
2. Take care to impart information concisely.
3. Remember there may be different levels of intelligence and/or dog training knowledge in the class.
4. Establish the right atmosphere.
5. Your pupils must not be afraid to ask questions so make them feel comfortable to do so.

6. Use tact sensitivity, intelligence, common-sense.
7. If someone misunderstands tell them it is your fault for not explaining properly.
8. Try and relax the class but do not be condescending or demean people.
9. Never reproach anyone for being late, remember their house may have burnt down or their mother may have died.
10. Remember that it is easier to make enemies than friends.
11. Develop a rapport with your class. Make everyone belong to the group.
12. If you unwittingly cause offence, apologise.

DON'TS

1. Don't worry about being nervous but worry if you are not.
2. Don't give the impression that simple questions should not have been asked.
3. Don't talk down or be patronising.
4. Don't presume others have too much knowledge for you to teach them.
5. Don't single out one person, treat all as equals.
6. Don't be a statue, act naturally and move around a little.
7. Don't tell risque, racist, religious, sexist, or political jokes.
8. Don't tread on people's dignity, you may offend them for life.
9. Don't make jokes about a pupils dog that may offend them.

END CONCLUSION

1. When possible compliment your class.
2. Cease on a good note.
3. Use handouts of notes where applicable.
4. Reinforce your teaching by a resume of the main points.
5. Above all be natural.
6. Always acknowledge those who taught you.

IN OTHER WORDS JUST BE THE PERFECT TEACHER

2

The Basis of Agility Instruction

It is not sufficient to accept any dog owner as a potential Agility handler without question. Certain points should first be ascertained to enable you to assess whether the dog is suitable for this sport. It does not end there for much should be explained to them regarding commands, signals and how important their body will be to the dog.

There is an argument for using this chapter as a basis for an informal lecture for new Agility handlers when they first attend. If you have digested the first chapter then we are sure that you will not forget the hand outs to reinforce your lecture. It should also be pertinent to include some explanation of the sport's structure in your particular country.

IS THE DOG SUITABLE FOR AGILITY?

1. Is he too young?
2. Is he fit?
3. Is he overweight?
4. Is he the right material?
5. Is he under control?
6. Is he of the right temperament?

AT WHAT AGE CAN THEY START?

In the U.K. the Kennel Club regulations quite rightly stipulate that a dog cannot be entered in Agility until he is 18 months of age. Originally the minimum age was 12 months but competitors were introducing into competition a fully trained Agility dog at 12 months which meant that they must have been training long before legal entry age.

It is difficult to generalise about the minimum age that dogs can be permitted to start training but some guidelines are appropriate. What must be borne in mind is that all the dogs bones should have matured and this varies with different breeds. Some of the larger heavier breeds bones do not mature until in excess of 15 months whilst others may be mature at 12 months. Always err on the side of caution but as a rough guide most Collies bones have matured at the age of 12 months whereas this is unlikely to have occurred in breeds such as German Shepherd Dogs until they have passed 15 months.

As well as physical immaturity in the young dog we have to consider the psychological age of a dog starting Agility. All too often we concern ourselves with the dog's bones and joints, and rightly so, but not to the exclusion of whether it is mentally ready. It is our belief that many crazy Agility dogs probably owe their condition to being taught at the wrong mental age. Agility, being the excitable and enjoyable sport that it is to most dogs, can easily lead a young puppy into believing that all there is to it is charging around out of control. Before the handler realises it they have a problem dog on their hands. They now try to exert discipline in an attempt to stop the young dog doing exactly what it has been allowed to do. The young dog's mental immaturity cannot cope with this drastic turn around in its handlers behaviour and there ensues a battle of wits between them. The results are there for all to see. Whilst at the training ground the handler can exert the type of compulsion now needed to make the dog obey, but once in competition that compulsion is totally ineffective and the dog reverts back to its puppyhood and behaves as it wishes. If the handler does eventually gain some form of competition control, the dog now behaves in such a way as to perform grudgingly.

Whilst some clubs will allow younger dogs to commence training on low obstacles we do not recommend this. It is all very well and good whilst an experienced instructor can supervise in a class situation, but what handlers do when they are elsewhere is another matter.

BASIC CONTROL

It is quite clear that obstacles are best taught to a dog that is under control. To attempt to teach Agility before this has been achieved is to invite confusion in the dog's mind and/or to store up problems for the future. There should be no question of running dogs around an Agility course on lead because this is the only way control can be maintained. In our opinion it is a recipe for disaster as it is not a short cut to quality work. Leads in Agility are an encumbrance serving only to help destroy a dog's balance and they need to be dispensed with quickly. This can only be done with a dog who is under control lead free.

Four basic control requirements for Agility are:-

1. 'Sit'

This is a general control factor for it is from this position that other control and Agility lessons often commence. As much basic obstacle instruction is best taught by recalling a dog, starting from the sit position is the most convenient. It is also the most commonly used position from which to start a competition run.

2. 'Down'

This command will not only be used on the table, and where it's immediate compliance saves valuable time, but also in Agility training an immediate down has many uses. Turn to the chapter on contact training for further details.

3. 'Wait'

As with sitting on command for basic obstacle teaching so is a 'Wait' necessary when teaching by recall. It is also necessary if freestyle handling is to be employed for the handler will wish to leave his dog in a 'Wait' on the start line. This same command may be used while the handler repositions himself while his dog is on the table, and it also occasionally has uses on difficult sections of the course. There is also a use in contact training.

4. Recall

It goes without saying that if basic obstacles are to be taught by recalling then the applicable command must first have been perfected on the control field. There are also many parts of an Agility course where a recall is an advantage, not least of all for the handler who wishes to call his dog over the first few jumps towards him.

Of much additional help is a dog who will:-

5. Run with their handler

Although heel work has little use on an Agility course, there are occasions when the command's immediate compliance can get a handler out of trouble. We do not however advocate it's use as a normal part of Agility handling.

6. Retrieve

So much can be taught to a dog who loves to play retrieve. The dog who will not return a thrown toy is frustrating to say the least, so therefore we recommend that pupils who are thought likely to become keen competitors should have this pointed out to them. If necessary much work should be done at home on encouraging the dog to play and also with a formal retrieve so that the dog learns that he must, at the very least, bring the article back and deliver to hand.

7. Sendaway

There are many instances on an Agility course where an ability to send the dog ahead is an advantage. This is where a pre-taught send away gives the dog confidence to work ahead of his handler. A send away in its strict Obedience competition form is not required, it is just the fact that the dog is used to working ahead of his handler. Many dogs, particularly those who have been trained for a lot of heel work, are reluctant to leave their handlers and therefore an ability to send away on command helps to overcome the problem.

All these control factors should be able to be achieved on one command but not with any kind of precision as required in other dog training disciplines such as Obedience competitions.

Summary:-

1. Sit.
2. Down.
3. Wait.
4. Recall.

Of much additional help is a dog who will:-

5. Run with their handler.
6. Retrieve.
7. Send away.

ASSESSING BASIC CONTROL

If we accept that new pupils should have basic control of their dogs before attempting Agility then a method of assessing control is required. Some dual Obedience and Agility clubs have standard progress tests for Obedience and therefore require pupils to pass at a certain level of Obedience as a method of determining when a dog is under sufficient control to commence Agility. Such systems are fine and if they work well for your club then we would not argue the point. There is however the possibility that under test a dog may luckily work far better than usual or, as is more likely to be the case, have a poor test.

Many Obedience classes are held indoors particularly in northern Europe whilst Agility classes are more likely to be outdoors. The way a dog responds away from the Obedience hall in which he is trained is often different and for these reasons we prefer an on the spot assessment. If the new dog and handler are taken into the area of an Agility class with all its attendant distractions the handler can either be asked to demonstrate what control they have or to do certain things with his dog.

We suggest that you ask the handler to tell the dog to sit, following this to go down. Then you can ask the handler to leave the dog so you can test whether he will wait and finally ask him to be recalled. All this can be done on the lead but the real test comes when you ask the handler to let his dog off the lead and to ignore him. Once you see the dog is suitably distracted with a good sniffing session or he has gone to see another dog that is the time to ask the handler to recall him. What happens during the next few seconds will give an indication of the handlers general control and it is a completely practical test. Watch for how many commands are required for these control facets particularly when the handler is calling his dog away from another. Remember to assess temperament to ensure that the dog is not nervous aggressive with people nor has any aggressive intentions to other dogs.

Summary:-

What you will be assessing is if the dog will :-

1. Sit
2. Down
3. Wait or stay
4. Recall on lead
5. Recall off lead when distracted.
6. Respond immediately to commands.

THE USE OF COMMANDS

Commands should be kept to a minimum. Do not let handlers develop the habit of incessant chatter to the dog. Commands used sparingly are more likely to be effective.

Agility commands are often used in conjunction with signals and/or body language. See pages 18 & 19.

Instructors from non English speaking countries who teach Agility in a different language should not necessarily use a literal translation from our suggested English commands. Such translations may not be suitable. For as all good trainers should know it is sounds that matter and each sound should be distinct from the other.

Commands can be broken down into three groups as follows:-

Control commands - Attention commands - Action commands

CONTROL COMMANDS

1. 'Sit'

Used at the start and for general control before and after entering the ring.

2. 'Wait'

Used at the start particularly if the handler is to leave the dog behind the line and take up position further along the course. It is also used effectively by some handlers to gain control on contact obstacles. Another use is at the table or pause while the handler repositions.

3. 'Steady'

Used at any time to slow the dog down and often to bring a dog more slowly down a contact obstacle.

4. 'Come'

The basic recall command which all dogs should understand. It is often used as a directional command when the dog is required to turn towards his handler, or simply to go straight to his handler.

5. 'Go on'

A good command for sending the dog on ahead.

6. 'This way'

While there are handlers who use this command just to get their dog to turn in their direction irrespective of the direction this manual teaches its use solely as a command to turn the dog right.

7. 'Back'

We recommend the use of this command to turn the dog left when he is working ahead.

8. 'Down'

Can be used at the start and at the table for the pause. During training this command will often be used particularly for basic training with tunnels. It also has a major use when teaching contacts (see Chapter 4.)

ATTENTION COMMANDS

An attention command has great value. We describe an attention command as one that immediately returns the dog's attention to his handler particularly when working on. For example, when a dog must jump then turn through 90 to 180 degrees to take the next obstacle. The most common use of this command is to follow it quickly with a directional signal.

1. Dog's name

If the dog has a short or maximum two syllable name then that name can be used as an attention command. However if in the past the dogs name has been delivered in a manner in which the dog has already learned not to immediately obey, reteaching it's use for Agility is necessary. To do so the dog must be taught to immediately turn towards his handler when his name is delivered in a special urgent fashion which may need to be also delivered with a change of pitch (usually higher). This must first be perfected away from the Agility area and not introduced into Agility until the dog is totally reliable with it's use.

2. 'Come'

Some handlers use 'Come' as an attention command but we would recommend an alternative word or the dogs name as described above. Most experienced dogs know that 'Come' used during Agility rounds does not necessarily mean that they must completely return to their handler. However it's use just as an attention command in Agility leaves the possibility of erroneously reteaching the dog that he does not have to completely return when the command is used in other circumstances.

3. 'Here'

An alternative is to use a command such as 'Here', but in every case work on the dog's immediate reaction to the command must be carried out before it is applied in Agility.

ACTION COMMANDS

This group refers to commands to be associated in the dog's mind as obstacle commands. Some handlers prefer to name every obstacle but from experience we have found this to be unnecessary except as a psychological boost for a minority of handlers.

It is not necessary to be pedantic about certain commands for certain obstacles and handlers can often be given a choice. There is however a argument for uniformity within a club if at any time handlers wish another club member to work their dog. However it will be seen from the suggestions below that some commands can be varied but once chosen they must be adhered to.

1. 'Up'

All hurdle type obstacles and contact obstacles. Some handlers also like to use this command for the long jump.

2. 'Jump'

All hurdle type obstacles. This command is really an alternative to the one above but is rarely used for contact obstacles as well. It can also be used for the long jump

3. 'Over'

Long jumps and water jumps. Some also like to use this for a spread jump. It is also favoured by some for hurdles.

4. 'Through'

All obstacles that the dog goes through such as the hoop (tyre), tunnels, weaving poles.

5. 'Walk on'

Used for dog walks, see-saws and 'A' ramps and is a command taken from the horse riding world.

6. 'Weave' or 'Poles'

As the names suggests this command is reserved exclusively for weaving as it really does not suit any other use.

Summary:-

CONTROL COMMANDS

1. 'Sit'
2. 'Wait'
3. 'Steady'
4. 'Come'
5. 'Go on'
6. 'This Way'
7. 'Back'
8. 'Down'

ATTENTION COMMANDS

1. Dog's name
2. 'Come'
3. 'Here'

ACTION COMMANDS

1. 'Up'
2. 'Jump'
3. 'Over'
4. 'Through'
5. 'Walk on'
6 . 'Weave' or 'Poles'

THE USE OF SIGNALS

Signals are an essential part of Agility and handlers should be taught their correct use from the beginning. For example during early basic obstacle lessons such as hurdles, arm signals should be employed.

Many handler's signals are not totally clear to their dogs and it is because they are not taught how to positively signal in the first place. Some basic rules about signals should be established with new handlers as soon as they are required to use them. As we recommend this to be during hurdle training it is likely that a handler's first or at least second lesson will require the use of arm signals.

For the purpose of this manual, when we talk about arm or hand signals we are referring to signals given by arm and hand. As a general guide all signals should be given by the arm nearest the dog. There are exceptions to this rule according to where a handler may be positioned in relation to his dog but it is better just to explain that signals are always given by the arm nearest the dog.

Signals must be given in a positive fashion, i.e. the arm should clearly be extended in a smooth but quick manner and held out for one or two seconds before being withdrawn.

Do not teach handlers to run around with their arms permanently extended for this dilutes the signal effect when really required. The permanently extended arm can be likened to a handler who talks incessantly to their dog who in effect never listens because all he hears is incessant chatter.

Handlers with good control can be taught to help their dogs become signal conscious. Teach this by sitting dog and handler opposite each other several feet or yards away in a 'Wait' position. The handler should then place a toy between himself and the dog but to one side before returning to his position. The handler then gives a positive signal towards the toy simultaneously giving the dog his retrieve command. The other side is taught as well and quickly the dog will learn the meaning of the signal.

This exercise can be taught in a living room while the handler remains seated. Alternatively it can be taught over greater distances outside.

Summary:-

1. Teach how signals should be given from early lessons.
2. Arm signals are hand signals as well.
3. Signals should usually be given by the arm nearest the dog.
4. Signals should be positively and clearly given.
5. An extended arm should not be left out during a round.
6. Teach handlers signal exercises using their dog's toy.

BODY LANGUAGE

Body language refers to the signals we give to others. The words were first used to describe an unspoken language between male and female but it applies more to dogs who understand the language our bodies convey. Dogs spend much of their time observing what we are doing so that they learn certain routines just by watching what our bodies do. Take the simple example of going to the cupboard where the biscuits are kept. This conveys a message to the dog. Take the biscuit tin out and the message becomes even more clear to the dog. We are therefore able to use our body to talk to our dogs but our body can convey the wrong messages if we do not understand what we are doing.

Of all the dog training disciplines Agility dogs pick up more from body movement than others. Instructors should therefore ensure that the maximum use is made of body language to assist handlers dogs and also to point out incorrect messages that are conveyed by poor body language.

In the first place it is usually necessary to tidy up a handler's body movement. Most new Agility handlers are ungainly to say the least. Some run around with their arms waving around like windmills. This not only conveys many unwanted messages but becomes like an unceasing chatter which the dog eventually takes no notice of. Others run in a wooden manner.

Previously we have dealt with signals. Now we must deal with correct positioning of the body in relation to the dog and body movements themselves. The dog will also pick up the sound of a handler's body movement when he cannot see him and this we must use to advantage. For instance when in the tunnel he will know by sound which side of the tunnel we are on. If we additionally use our voice this reinforces his perception of where we are in relation to him. We can use this to great advantage by positioning our body in such a place that when he exits from a tunnel he is moving in the direction in which we require.

In situations where the dog is working ahead but will have to subsequently chose between working on or turning left or right to jump, the position of our body, backed up by command, is of paramount importance.

A good example of body movements conveying an incorrect message is when a handler moves too quickly away from a contact obstacle. He transmits the wrong body language to a dog who will undoubtedly jump off as his handler moves, hence many dogs learn to prematurely leave contact obstacles.

There are many other instances but at this stage of a new handler's learning it is sufficient to tidy up their body language and make them aware of the messages their bodies can convey to their dog.

Ensure that handlers are aware of:-

1. Poor body movement conveying false messages.
2. How much information their dog will glean from body movement.
3. Their body position being crucial at all times, conveying right or wrong messages to their dog.
4. That good signals, commands and body language combined leave little doubt in the dogs mind about a handlers requirements.

RIGHT & LEFT HANDLING

The basis of freestyle handling is an ability of dog and handler to work together no matter where either one is placed. Right from the very first obstacle lessons new pupils must be made to handle at each obstacle from either side. Those that have spent time in other dog disciplines at first find it very uncomfortable when their dog is on their right hand side. It is only psychological and soon overcome providing they persevere. The dog also needs to know that he must not always come to the heel side. It is quite easy to attain providing that from early hurdle lessons handling is taught from both sides.

For those handlers who say they cannot get their dog to work on their right hand side, ask them to sit their dog at heel, then tell him to 'Wait' while they move and stand beside him on the other side so that he is on their right. From here they should instruct the dog to jump a hurdle. As they progress, and when they reach the applicable stage, they should be able to run towards the hurdle with the dog on either side. It is then a matter of continuing this approach at every obstacle. Ensure that they do not rigidly alternate the sides the dog starts from but rather randomly chose sides such as two starts right, one left, one right, two left etc.

Summary:-

1. Handling right and left is taught from the beginning.
2. With the dog in a 'Sit Wait' the handler should change sides.
3. Ensure handling side changes are selected randomly.
4. All obstacles should have this double sided handling approach.

TRAINING EQUIPMENT

Whilst good quality competition Agility equipment is a great asset to a club there are other additional items that are useful.

1.   For initial teaching a hurdle without wings allows handlers to pass closer to the hurdle on all initial training stages.

2.   A scaffold plank with 12" (305 mm) high wire mesh fixed to the sides is useful for teaching dogs to run up and down a plank without worry. (See chapter 3 on dog walk training).

3.   Hoops as assistance for early contact training or retraining the dog to a new method. (See Chapter 4 on Hoops).

4.   Whilst contact equipment should be very stable for learner dogs it is a good idea to have some less stable obstacles so that experienced dogs are exposed to them in training. In such a way dogs will not be surprised when encountering unfamiliar and unstable contact obstacles.

5.   A good selection of broom handles of suitable lengths and possibly a training weave frame are necessary additions to standard equipment. (See Chapter 3 on weaving poles).

6.   A lower table for mini dog training which can be used as a step to the higher table is an advantage.

Summary:-

    1. A hurdle without wings for learner dogs.
    2. A scaffold plank with wire mesh for alternative plank training.
    3. Hoops for contact work.
    4. Broom handles and training weave equipment.
    5. A mini height table.

TEACHING PLAY

Amazing though it may seem many dog owners never consider teaching their dogs how to play. Most dogs will play by instinct but not all will. We are great believers in teaching young puppies how to play and this definitely includes those that will play naturally.

Whilst Agility is play for dogs many facets of it can be taught by the use of a toy. New pupils need to be assessed for their dogs ability to play and, where necessary, they must be taught. For some people prancing about with a dog is embarrassing. To the dog someone who is going to leap about is much more fun than a staid handler.

First of all ensure that you bring your handlers alive to the extent that they become animated and that their voice becomes interesting to a dog. For many dogs this becomes a game in itself but they will be in the minority. To ensure that handlers are going to have an easy means of motivation teaching the dog to play with toys is what you really require. To do this get your erring handler on hands and knees and show them how to excite the dog with a toy, tug or ball, occasionally throwing it a few feet to attempt play retrieves. If the dog is likely to run off with the toy then these games should be played while the dog is confined by a lead.

It may be necessary, indeed we consider it to be good practise, for the dog to be taught to retrieve and in this context you will need to refer applicable handlers to an Obedience class that includes retrieve teaching. A playful dog can be taught practically anything by play. Doing so will result in a dog who has learned by fun without being placed under stress.

Summary:-

    1. Animate the handler.
    2. Ensure their voice is interesting to the dog.
    3. Encourage them to have play sessions at home with toys or tugs.
    4. Emphasise how dogs can be taught by play.

PRAISE AND REWARD

The use of praise and reward is a basic principal of all dog training yet is often overlooked by instructors. To quickly teach their dog that his actions meet with approval a handler must understand that praise must be used instantaneously with the required action. The level of praise must be adjusted to the dog and for one that is very excitable praise levels might need to be kept low. For the bored dog praise should be expansive.

Beware of handlers that over use praise, incorrectly time praise, or praise the dog because they have been told to but do so at inappropriate times. Praise incorrectly used has no positive use whatsoever.

Remember that rewards can be used together with praise or just on their own. There are many Agility training instances where thrown toys can be used and of course food can also be used as a reward and this subject is dealt with next.

Summary:-

1. Praise must be instantaneous with a required action.
2. Praise level should be adjusted to suit the dog.
3. Watch for incorrectly timed praise.
4. Look out for inappropriate praise.
5. Incorrectly given praise has no use at all.

THE USE OF FOOD

The advantages of using food to train animals has been well known by experts for many years; it is one of the quickest ways in which to gain an animals confidence and, if used correctly, can relay an instant message to a dog that he has performed well. During initial obstacle teaching tit-bits can be of great use and they can also be used later to reinforce training methods such as contacts. When used as inducement to teach a new dog the golden rule should be to give the dog the tit-bit the instant he completes his task. This means the tit-bit must be ready without having to search through pockets of rubbish or open a bag in order to deliver the treat. The vital seconds immediately after the dog has performed are crucial and generally this is where most handlers tend to get it wrong. While they are fumbling for a tit-bit, in a bag contained in their pocket, the dogs attention has wavered and the opportunity to reinforce good behaviour has been lost.

When food is being used to tempt a dog to negotiate a contact point or to go through a tunnel, pupils should be taught how to hold a tit-bit. It sounds silly doesn't it but if, for instance, a tit-bit is placed in the palm of the hand it is likely that the dog can take it before he should and therefore he has no need to perform. On the other hand if the tit-bit is concealed too well the dog may never know of it's presence and therefore the inducement factor is severely lowered. We have always found that the best way to hold a tit-bit is between thumb and forefinger, in this way it can be used as a lure without the dog being able to take it until it is given.

The instructor must be ever vigilant on the over use or incorrect use of tit-bits by pupils. When a dog is so besotted by reward to the exclusion of what he should be doing the handler has got it wrong during teaching. He must now be advised accordingly before the habit becomes too difficult to break. This does not necessarily mean abandon the use of tit-bits but it does mean that they should be used more sparingly and with correct timing.

Summary:-

1. Tit-bits can be used for initial obstacle teaching.
2. Tit-bits can also be used for contact training.
3. Tit-bits should be ready in the hand.
4. Tit-bits must be given instantly the task is completed.
5. Tit-bits should be held by finger and thumb.
6. Tit-bits must not be over used.

CORRECTION

When, where, how ?

It is our belief that correction and Agility are opposites. Far too many dogs are corrected on Agility training courses when the root of the problem is lack of basic control. This can result in the dog being nervous of the handler, frightened of equipment and hesitant in performing. He will become confused about his handlers requirement which is likely to result in a dog that will make even more mistakes in an effort to please, or perform in an unhappy manner.

In our opinion, and many other enlightened dog trainers, a dog taught by compulsion will seldom perform in a happy and enjoyable manner, and in moments of stress will revert back to his demeanour when taught. We therefore strongly advocate that a dog should not be put under stress when teaching Agility.

If the problem is basic control, the dog should be educated away from Agility equipment. This may mean advising the handler to attend Obedience classes until a necessary amount of control has been established.

If the handler normally has basic control but it is Agility equipment that causes a breakdown of control, the problem will inevitably be due to incorrect initial teaching. Special exercises can be employed to combat this. Control work such as 'SIT', 'DOWN', 'WAIT', 'COME', and 'LEAVE' should be used on the Agility field without the dog being allowed to negotiate any equipment. If the handler is entering competitions a complete break for several months should be advised in conjunction with control training. On no account must the handler be allowed to use harsh handling and he should, if at all possible, be supervised totally by one instructor until some improvement around the equipment has been established.

Summary:-

1. Correction and Agility are opposites.
2. Compulsion will not produce a happy Agility dog.
3. Continual correction shows a lack of basic control.
4. No control on Agility equipment means revert to basic exercises.

AGILITY TRAINING

How much, how often?

We are constantly being asked how much training a dog should be given. It is extremely difficult to generalise without seeing the dog in question. What is too much for one dog may not nearly be enough for another, so what should be considered is the dogs age, experience, general disposition, breed, size and fitness. Also paramount in the instructor's mind should be quality not quantity of training employed, and an instructor should never be afraid to advise a handler when to stop. Instructors must make it their business to keep a watchful eye on handlers who tend to over train their dog.

Remember it is better to finish any training session 10 minutes early when a dog is working well than to continue ten minutes too long and invite mistakes brought about by lack of attention or enthusiasm. Sometimes during a training session all a dog may need to revive his interest is a short break of play or rest; it is the good instructor who can recognise when this point has been reached.

Summary:-

1. Do not allow over training.
2. Assess to determine when the dog's limit has been reached.
3. Stop a pupil training before his dog's limit is reached.
4. Ensure training is quality rather than quantity.
5. Insist upon the dog having rest or play.

USING THE TRAINING LEAD

During initial obstacle training, if used correctly, the lead can play a vital part in establishing a solid learning foundation. Used incorrectly results can be seen months and even years later as the root cause of a dogs problems. If a dog is kept on a lead during training rounds because lead free control has not been established, one result will be that the dog will almost certainly always jump at an angle towards his handler. This happens because lead tightening has occurred during jumping. In order to keep their dog on line for the next obstacle a handler will probably do an about turn with his dog, thus teaching jump, turn around, then jump again. Even when the dog may possibly be able to work lead free, if this method is employed for any length of time, the natural tendency for that dog on a course will be to crash into his handler's left leg after each jump. He will probably circle before the next one, and turn to the right just before a left turn.

This type of dog will also be one who crowds his handler on contact equipment, often coming off the side at an angle. He will knock down hurdle poles because his natural jumping style has been inhibited, and will rarely work on ahead. All of these problems will be difficult, sometimes impossible, to cure so instructors are strongly advised never to allow such a mistake to occur in the first place.

Summary:-

1. Good initial lead work will lay a good foundation.
2. Extensive Agility lead training may cause later problems.

DISPENSING WITH LEADS

Knowledgeable instructors will know just when a pupil should dispense with a lead. This will usually be when the dog is proficient on an obstacle and a lead's use is becoming more of a hindrance than a help. There may come a time later when a lead can be re-employed for a specific purpose.

This may be reinforcing contact training, helping a dog if it's confidence has been lowered on a particular obstacle, or using a longer lead for teaching quicker turn rounds after jumping. Generally speaking we believe that leads should be dispensed with as quickly as possible.

Summary:-

1. Dispense with leads as soon as possible.

AVOIDING ANTICIPATION LEARNING

Great care should be taken by instructors that they recognise when anticipation is being taught. Having been shown what is required many dogs quickly learn what comes next and, in their desire to please, commence the next part before instructed to do so. This type of enthusiasm from a new dog is of course desirable but, if unaware of consequences, should anticipation continue a pupil can easily make this into an insurmountable problem. Unfortunately the very nature of Agility relies upon anticipation, but being able to leave a dog on the start line or table without anticipation is a great asset to an Agility handler.

The problem can either start the very first time a dog is placed in front of an obstacle, or after a few weeks training as he gains more confidence. Having been commanded to wait, the dog, in his enthusiasm, flinches a muscle and the handler calls him. In a matter of just a few training sessions he learns how to anticipate his handler's command by a split second. After a few more training sessions the dog even anticipates long before his handler even thinks of giving the command. After yet more training sessions his anticipation learning has reached such a high level of perfection that he can now take off at the slightest movement of his handler's body.

Avoidance of anticipation learning should be uppermost in instructor's minds when dealing with inexperienced handlers and their dogs. Handlers should never command their dog to negotiate an obstacle when it is the dog that has decided the time is right to do so. If that is likely to happen, it is just prior to such an instance that the handler should repeat his 'Wait' command and, if necessary, return to the dog without allowing him to move. For a dog already proficient at anticipation this exercise may have to used many times.

Pupils should also be informed about the importance of body movements when a dog is waiting. Remember it is desirable to have a dog responding to body signals, but all too often new handlers have no idea that they are relaying body signals to their dogs.

Summary:-

1. Watch for anticipation at starts and table pause.
2. Anticipation must be stopped quickly.
3. 'Wait' should be repeated if anticipation looks likely.
4. Where necessary a dog must be returned to and not called.

FOOTWEAR AND CLOTHING

Many club instructors will already be aware of the differing attire that dog owners wear at their first training session, much of it being inappropriate to dog training.

Bad footwear is anything that may harm a dog such as spiked shoes, heavy boots or high heels. Unsuitable clothing is anything that flaps which may make an already nervous dog more so. Flapping clothing can give inapplicable signals to a dog or prevent his handler from seeing him.

In short, handlers should wear something comfortable on their feet, training shoes are ideal, waterproof boots or short boots if wet, and no loose fitting garments that are undone should be worn. Handlers should be aware of how slippery grass can be, particularly early in the morning which is not as obvious as when rain has fallen. Trainer shoes with studs are ideal in such conditions allowing handlers to make quick turns safely.

Summary:-

1. Ensure footwear is suitable
2. Ensure clothing is suitable.
3. For wet grass trainers with rubber studs are best.

INITIAL TRAINING COMMANDS

In our experience we have not found it necessary to introduce commands until a dog is actually negotiating the obstacle without problem. In the long term introducing a command too early may well have the reverse effect to that which was intended.

A dog placed in front of a low hurdle and recalled over by his name and recall command is all that is needed to effect a result. A dog placed at the entrance of a short tunnel and subsequently recalled will achieve the required result. A dog helped over an 'A' ramp by handler and instructor, or recalled by the handler from the apex using encouragement and his name will nearly always achieve the desired effect.

Once a dog has learned what is required, commands can be introduced. Using eventual obstacle commands too early can cause two different problems. A dog that is given a command before it knows what is required has its first chance to refuse that command. A dog that has a bad experience with an obstacle may associate the given command with that bad experience and retain that association for ever.

Summary:-

1. Do not introduce commands to your pupils too soon.
2. Avoid wrong association of ideas.

GOOD TRAINING CLASS PRACTICE

A well run training class should be enjoyable for the dogs, handlers, instructor and even spectators. The greatest danger is letting the fun element of Agility overshadow the serious business of training, for one has to assume that people train their dogs to improve them. This does not mean that classes should be so formal as to exclude fun, indeed we have always advocated that Agility and fun go hand in hand.

A few simple rules that everyone knows and understands will be of great benefit to any training class. With the exception of those with much experience, handlers and dogs should not be allowed to use equipment without supervision and the instructor should be in a position to oversee at all times. When not working all dogs should be on lead and kept quiet so that they are not a nuisance to anyone else.

Harsh handling should never be allowed or encouraged by anyone, and where possible classes should be kept to dogs of similar ability. Inexperienced or young dogs put amongst the club's best can invite a handler to put unnecessary pressure on their dog.

It is also a problem placing dogs that cannot yet successfully tackle obstacle sequences in amongst dogs capable of complete rounds. This will tend to disrupt class flow and inhibit progress for the advanced dogs.

The way in which a class is run ultimately remains the instructors responsibility, and therefore an example in behaviour should be set by being punctual, understanding, caring, prepared, and above all be seen to be in charge without being dictatorial.

In this day and age of anti dog people it is also our opinion that club instructors should be first to insist that handlers 'pick up' their dogs droppings both at club and when exercising.

Summary:-

1. Treat training seriously.
2. At the same time retain the fun element.
3. Make simple rules that everyone understands.
4. Never allow harsh handling.
5. Try and keep classes to dogs of similar ability.
6. Set an example of behaviour.
7. Be seen to be in charge without being a dictator.
8. Insist that handlers 'pick up' that which their dogs drop.

THE DO'S & DON'TS OF TRAINING

Instructors should always be on the lookout for handlers who unwittingly employ poor and ultimately detrimental training methods. Do not allow them to jump their dog back and forth over the same obstacle which will soon instil a 'back jumping' habit.

When working for a period on one obstacle do not allow handlers to repeatedly call their dog back for one attempt after another. This only teaches jump and turn back as a habit and does not encourage a dog to 'Work on'.

Take care to give good advice to a handler who allows his dog to continually 'take it's own course' in the name of fun. After a few weeks, when fun has worn a little thin, they will be asking you how to stop it and the best way of stopping a fault is to never allow it to occur in the first place.

For dog training instructors the handler who is impatient has always been a problem. Care must be taken to impart advice in such a way that will not dampen their enthusiasm nor impair their dogs well-being and long term progress.

With competition in mind all new handlers should be encouraged to teach their dog each obstacle from both handling sides. It is easy to become so wrapped up with initial teaching so that telling or reminding them of the importance of this good training practice is forgotten. It is something both instructor and handler may later regret.

Another question you will wish to avoid after a handler has been attending training classes for a few months is "how do I stop my dog barking on the Agility course" ? You must impress upon new handlers that barking during initial teaching must be discouraged without dampening enthusiasm, for if it continues it will be very hard to stop later.

Summary:-

1. Watch out for poor handling methods.
2. Do not allow handlers to jump dogs back and forth.
3. Do not allow handlers to jump the dog and call him back.
4. Do not allow dogs to start taking their own course.
5. Watch out for impatient handlers.
6. Initial obstacle training should be from both handling sides.
7. Stop course barking developing from the beginning.

MISTAKES MEAN REVERT

A golden rule for all dog training is that if the dog is making mistakes on a new teaching sequence the handler should be told to go back to a previously successful stage. Once sure the dog has regained confidence and knows exactly what is required an attempt can be made to proceed to the next stage again.

Summary:-

1. Revert to the previous stage when mistakes are being made.
2. Do not progress the handler again until the dog is perfect at the previous stage and has had considerably more confidence building practise.

TRAINING CLASS STRUCTURE

What often determines Agility class training structure is the number of obstacles available and number of pupils attending. If you have a small class of experienced handlers and dog with one set of equipment, individual obstacles can be practised in conjunction with sequences of several obstacles together. If time and numbers permit, a complete course at the beginning or end of the session can be used. In our experience just training on complete rounds can do more harm than good. Always allow some time during a class to pay particular attention to individual handler problems. Having ascertained their problems consider likely cures, but be prepared for the experienced handler's standard reply, "I've tried that and it doesn't work"!

The two other groups that the instructor is likely to encounter are newcomers looking at Agility for the first time and inexperienced handlers who still need a great deal of help. Whilst both of these groups will require attention, newcomers will undoubtedly take the lions share of an instructors precious time.

For newcomers a solid foundation of obstacle training is essential before progress can be made towards linking a sequence of obstacles together. With early learners it is therefore a good idea for the same instructor to take this class so that he can keep a record of each dog's progress and plan training sessions accordingly.

Those dogs who have learned negotiation of the obstacles should now progress to obstacle sequencing. Again it is essential for instructors to have planned their training session in advance in order to give pupils maximum training time benefit. This avoids getting stuck in a rut by repeating routines week after week. At the end of a training session handlers should be taught to appreciate the efforts made on their behalf by being actively encouraged to help put equipment away. It is always difficult to lay down hard and fast guidelines about training class structure, for each club varies in the amount of obstacles they have and number of pupils.

Summary:-

1. Adapt classes to numbers of pupils and obstacles available.
2. Ascertain problems and consider likely cures.
3. Keep records of pupils progress.
4. Plan training sessions.
5. Teach handlers to help put equipment away.

AN INSTRUCTORS DOG

Great care should be taken when the need may arise to demonstrate a particular point with your own dog. There may be a danger of over using your dog, resulting in boredom or mistakes creeping in because you are demonstrating to others and not concentrating totally on handling. There is also a possibility that newcomers might think that the instructor is merely showing off and consequently the demonstrations point is lost. A far better method is to ask an experienced handler to demonstrate while you discuss the whys and wherefores with your class, answering any questions that may arise.

Summary:-

1. Take care not to over use your own dog for demonstrations.
2. Do not show off with your dog.
3. Ask another capable handler to demonstrate while you discuss.

EXPLANATIONS TO HANDLERS

All explanations from instructor to handler must be carried out before the dog is positioned for an attempt at an obstacle. The reasons for this are simple, the dog should not be left in a 'Wait' while a long explanation is given for this will encourage anticipation or boredom. Once a dog has been set up in a 'Wait' giving an explanation will divert the handler's attention away from his dog. During this time it is likely that the dog will move or at best become distracted, therefore explanation before set up is essential.

Some dogs become apprehensive of a new obstacle if too much fuss is made of preparing for an attempt. Far better that the explanation is given a small distance away from the obstacle and then subsequently indicate where an immediate attempt should be made from.

Whilst encompassing relevant points, ideally all instructors explanations should be brief. They should be addressed to the whole class while remembering that too much detail will not be taken in by most handlers. After each attempt by handler and dog there will inevitably be further points to add depending on how the attempt was carried out.

Summary:-

1. Explanations should be given before the dog is set up.
2. Handlers attention to their dog after set up is imperative.
3. Give the explanation away from the obstacle.
4. Keep initial explanations brief.
5. Give further advice after an attempt.

THE INSTRUCTORS BAG

All good instructors should have their own bag of training aids that should contain everything that may be needed during a training session. Handlers rarely have the right equipment for training, and an instructor who can produce all requirements on the spot as required is an instructor who has put some thought into his training session. Likely training aids the instructor's bag should contain are a soft collar, webbing or leather lead, an assortment of toys, ring, ball, sock, squeaky toy, tit-bits and other favourite items. Training bag apart, the instructor should also make sure that a first aid kit, suitable for dogs and handlers, is available at each training session.

Summary:-

Make sure that you have the following available:-

1. Soft collar.
2. Webbing or leather lead.
3. Assortment of toys, ring, ball, sock, squeaky toy.
4. Tit-bits.
5. Other favourite items.

PREPARING A PUPPY FOR AGILITY

Most handlers cannot wait to get started in Agility, even if their puppy is only a few months old. It is the instructor's responsibility to give correct advice on what a handler should be doing to prepare his puppy. Usually it is an inexperienced handler with his second or subsequent dog that is the most impatient, and more often than not he will somehow manage to achieve the same mistakes with a new dog as with his previous dogs. So what advice can the instructor give the handler with a new young puppy?

1. Basic control should not and cannot be overlooked if later Agility training is to be successful.
2. A lead is probably the most important training aid, and all basic training should be carried on lead to avoid the puppy making mistakes. If he does he will be learning that there is another way to do something and it will be THE WRONG WAY.
3. Teach the puppy to play with you rather than to play on his own.
4. Whilst playing introduce control that you know will be needed later.
5. Teach the puppy a perfect recall.
6. Teach the puppy to sit.
7. Teach the puppy to wait.
8. Teach the puppy to retrieve to hand.
9. Teach the puppy an instant down.
10. Socialise the puppy with dogs and humans.
11. Stop the puppy barking while playing with you from day one.
12. Always give the puppy a lot of your time alone.
13. Exercise and train the puppy on its own, not with other dogs in the same household.
14. Do not let the puppy spend too much time with your other dogs to the exclusion of yourself.
15. You should be building up a relationship of attention between you and your puppy, and not inadvertently condoning a reliance on your other dogs.

Introducing a young puppy to Agility obstacles has not proved to be necessary for success, indeed research may yet prove how much of an unwise practice this is. A puppy given a solid foundation of basic control and taught to be responsive and attentive to its handler, will bring success in any canine pursuit.

3

Teaching the Obstacles

New Agility pupils find some obstacles imposing. As a good instructor you will know that, with the exception of weaving poles, dogs can quickly learn to master each obstacle. The dog's confidence in his handler and his ability to tackle obstacles must soon be established, and this is where sound and knowledgeable instruction will set handler and dog off on the right path.

HURDLES

Always commence with a new pupil by teaching them hurdle training. This is the basis of Agility, for dogs are always required to jump hurdle type obstacles more often than any other. Hurdle training should not be rushed and it should be taught using just a single bar at a low height. It is always easier to ask a dog that is under control to recall to his handler, and this is therefore our recommended method of initial training. Raising the single bar is a critical factor and instructors should not allow enthusiastic newcomers to do so too soon.

INSTRUCTOR'S USE OF THE HURDLE AND TEACHING PROCEDURE

1. Preferably a hurdle without wings should be used. Wings are too clumsy for beginners.
2. A single bar should be set at a low height.
3. Teaching the hurdle should commence using the recall method.
4. The dog should be positioned in front of the hurdle at the best distance taking account of the bars height and dog's size.
5. When moving the handler to recall their dog the handler should preferably walk around a wingless hurdle. If the hurdle has wings they may step over the bar.

EXPLANATION FROM INSTRUCTOR TO HANDLER

Tell the handler:-

1. To sit the dog facing the hurdle.
2. The lead clip should be under the dogs chin.
3. A command 'Wait' is to be given simultaneously with a flat hand signal.
4. To move to the other side of the hurdle without turning their back on their dog.
5. The lead must be kept slack while moving into position.
6. Pause before calling the dog to avoid anticipation learning.
7. Use the dogs recall command, not a jump command.
8. Simultaneously call the dog and step back.
9. Step back bring your hands, holding the lead, to the groin.
10. Praise and reward where applicable.

LIKELY PROBLEMS

Problem - The dog anticipated the jump. What advice will you give?
Solution - If temperament allows I will hold the dog back by the collar but also advise more work on 'Wait' control.

Problem - The dog would not attempt to jump. What would you do?
Solution - Instruct handler to encourage with tit-bit or toy.

Problem - The dog knocked the pole down. What kind of correction would you advise?
Solution - None.

TRAINING PROGRESSION

1. Introduce the handlers chosen command.
2. Show how hand signals should be used from now on.
3. Handler to run with the dog on his left whilst his dog jumps.
4. Handler to run with the dog on his right whilst his dog jumps.
5. Dispense with the lead before proceeding further.
6. Running both sides with dog being encouraged by hand signal and command to jump ahead without handler.
7. Running (both sides) and sending the dog slightly ahead to jump using a toy. For an excitable dog a calmer situation can prevail if the instructor places the toy on the far side of the hurdle.
8. Raise the single bar as the dog learns and gains confidence.
9. Recalling the dog over the bar should be continued to be practised at all progression stages.

HOOP (TYRE)

Training for this obstacle should never be carried out until hurdle technique has been mastered. It is easier to teach by recalling the dog towards his handler whose face should be totally visible to his dog through the tyre. If not there is a danger of the dog going under the tyre or jumping to the side.

INSTRUCTOR'S USE OF THE HOOP AND TEACHING PROCEDURE

1. The hoop (tyre) should be lowered as far as possible.
2. The dog should be positioned in front of the tyre at the best distance taking account of tyre height and dog's size.

EXPLANATION FROM INSTRUCTOR TO HANDLER

Tell the handler:-

1. To sit the dog facing the tyre.
2. The lead clip is to be under the dogs chin.
3. A command 'Wait' is to be given simultaneously with a flat hand signal.
4. Pass the lead through the tyre (The instructor may do this).
5. Move to the far side without turning your back on the dog.
6. If necessary give further 'Wait' commands whilst moving.
7. Get right down so that your face is framed in the tyre.
8. Hold the lead with both hands slightly through the tyre.
9. Call the dog towards you while moving back.
10. Simultaneously use a recall command not a jump command.
11. Praise and reward if applicable.

LIKELY PROBLEMS

Problem - Dog refuses to go through tyre?
Solution - Use tit-bit or toy to encourage the dog through.

Problem - Dog tried to go either side of tyre?
Solution - Keep lead shorter so this is impossible.

Problem - Dog would not 'Wait' until handler moved to far side?
Solution - Instructor to hold collar but advise more 'Wait' training.

TRAINING PROGRESSION

1. Start by gradually raising tyre height.
2. Introduce the handler's chosen tyre command.
3. Send dog through using a command and hand signal.
4. Vary handling sides.
5. Run towards the tyre with the dog and ask him to jump it.
   Remember to use both handling sides.
6. If the dog is not too excitable throw a toy once he has landed.
   This should be done as a reward which will help gain confidence
   and speed.

FLEXIBLE PIPE TUNNEL

It is not necessary to teach the hurdle or hoop before this obstacle as both
tunnels have little to do with jumping. The same recall principle of
training applies using the logic of making it easy for the dog. One worry
with tunnels is that many dogs quickly grow to like them and, having got
to the stage where the dog is being sent through, he will start to go through
tunnels of his own accord. This must not be allowed.

INSTRUCTOR'S USE OF THE FLEXIBLE PIPE TUNNEL
AND TEACHING PROCEDURE

1. Pipe tunnels are always taught before collapsible tunnels.
2. Commence by closing it so that it is as short as possible.
3. The dog's starting position must be as close to the tunnel entrance
   as possible.
4. Down or sit should be used for a starting position according to size
   and the handler's control.
5. The instructor will remain with the dog.

EXPLANATION FROM INSTRUCTOR TO HANDLER

Tell the handler:-

1. To position the dog in front of the tunnel.
2. Give a command 'Wait' simultaneously with a flat hand signal.
3. Go to the far end.
4. If necessary give further 'Wait' commands whilst moving.
5. Your face must be framed in the tunnel exit.
6. I will pass the lead through to you.
7. Call the dog with a recall command.
8. Also use encouragement, tit-bit or toy.
9. Do not drag the dog through.
10. Praise and reward if applicable.

LIKELY PROBLEMS

Problem - He tried to go around the tunnel to get to his handler.
Solution - Make sure the dog could see the handler before he was called. The lead should be used to restrain him if necessary.

Problem - The dog could see his handler but he would not move.
Solution - Make greater use of encouragement tit-bits and toys.

Problem - The dog will not move when tit-bits or toys are used.
Solution - Tell the handler to go towards the dog by entering the tunnel.

TRAINING PROGRESSION

1. Start to lengthen the tunnel as the dog becomes confident.
2. When full length is achieved make a gentle bend in the tunnel.
3. Introduce the handler's chosen command for tunnels.
4. The handler should now send the dog using a command and signal then run ahead of the dog whilst encouraging him.
5. A thrown toy as the dog exits should be used to encourage speed and confidence. For excitable dogs this should not be done.
6. Right and left handling should now be used
7. Running and sending the dog slightly ahead to enter the tunnel. Both handling sides and a toy should continue to be used.
8. Go on to the collapsible tunnel and use the same method.

COLLAPSIBLE TUNNEL

Once the dog has come to understand what he should do at the pipe tunnel this one is quickly taught. Ideally an instructors assistant to hold the canvass open can be helpful.

INSTRUCTOR'S USE OF THE COLLAPSIBLE TUNNEL AND TEACHING PROCEDURE

1. Use an assistant if possible.
2. Start by using exit end method (See Method 'A' following).
3. The assistant's job will be to hold the material open and to keep it pulled tight into a tube.
4. The dog's starting position must be as close to the tunnel entrance as possible.
5. The down or sit should be used for a starting position according to size and control of dog.
6. The instructor should remain with the dog and hold his collar if necessary.

7. If method 'A' is unsuccessful use method 'B' see below.
8. Fold up the material to make the tunnel as short as possible.
9. The assistant will continue to hold the exit open & tight.

METHOD 'A' - Using the exit as the entrance

EXPLANATION FROM INSTRUCTOR TO HANDLER.

Tell the handler:-

1. To position the dog in front of the tunnel exit.
2. Give a command 'Wait' simultaneously with a flat hand signal.
3. Go to the far end.
4. If necessary give further 'Wait' commands whilst moving.
5. Your face must be framed in the tunnel entrance.
6. Call the dog with a recall command.
7. Use encouragement, tit-bit or toys if necessary.
8. Praise and reward if applicable.

TRAINING PROGRESSION

1. After several successful attempts using the exit as an entrance use the same procedure but from the correct entrance as described in method 'B' below.

METHOD 'B' - Folded material method

EXPLANATION FROM INSTRUCTOR TO HANDLER.

Tell the handler:-

1. To position the dog in front of the tunnel entrance.
2. Give a command 'Wait' simultaneously with a flat hand signal.
3. Go to the far end.
4. If necessary give further 'Wait' commands whilst moving.
5. Your face must be framed in the tunnel exit.
6. Call the dog with a recall command.
7. Use encouragement, tit-bit or toys if necessary.
8. Praise and reward if applicable.

LIKELY PROBLEMS

Problem - Dog tried to go around the tunnel to get to his handler?
Solution - Ensure the dog can see his handler before he is called.

Problem - The dog could see his handler but he would not move?
Solution - Make greater use of encouragement tit-bits and toys.

Problem - The dog definitely will not move when tit-bits or toys are
used.
Solution - Tell the handler to enter the tunnel and go towards his dog.

TRAINING PROGRESSION

1. Start to lengthen the tunnel as the dog becomes confident.
2. When the full length is achieved start to drop the material just prior
to him exiting.
3. Continue to drop the material progressively earlier until it is
unnecessary for the tunnel to be held open at all.
4. Introduce the handler's chosen command for tunnels.
5. Handler now to send dog using command and signal, then run
ahead of the dog encouraging so that their voice is ahead of him.
6. A thrown toy as the dog exits should be used to encourage speed
and confidence. For excitable dogs this should not be done.
7. Right and left handling should now be used.
8. Running and sending the dog slightly ahead to enter the tunnel
while continuing to use the toy.

TABLE

This is another obstacle that is obviously best trained once the dog has
mastered hurdle jumping and yet again recall methods are best.

INSTRUCTOR'S USE OF THE TABLE AND TEACHING PROCEDURE

1. The table is taught after the hurdle has been mastered.
2. Priority is given to getting the dog on the table. The down is taught
on the ground and is not necessarily used at this stage.
3. The table should be taught as a recall
4. Use a mini height table in front of the large one if necessary.
5. The instructor should assist when applicable by holding the lead.
6. Ask the handler to use a toy or tit-bit if necessary.
7. If tit-bits are to be used they must not be placed on the table; they will
encourage the dog under training ,and others, to sniff on the table.

EXPLANATION FROM INSTRUCTOR TO HANDLER

Tell the handler:-

1. Give the lead to me and go to the far side of the table.
2. Lean over the table and extend your hands and arms towards the dog while giving your recall command.
3. Encourage your dog up to you and lean back as he gets on.
4. Your dog must not be allowed to run around or under the table.
5. Do not allow your dog to jump straight off.
6. Praise and reward if applicable.

LIKELY PROBLEMS

Problem - The dog will not get on the table with his handler on the far side ?

Solution - Ask the handler to kneel on the back edge and proceed as before.

Problem - The dog still refuses to get on the table although his handler is kneeling on it.

Solution - Ask handler to stand on the back edge and proceed as before.

Problem - The dog is still very difficult, what else can be done ?

Solution - Place the hurdle in front of the table to encourage the dog to jump up.

Problem - The dog is having difficulty because of his size.

Solution - Use a lower table if available.

TRAINING PROGRESSION

1. Introduce the handler's chosen command for the table.
2. Handler to approach the table with their dog on lead giving command and signal to jump up.
3. Handler and dog to approach the table lead free giving command and signal to jump up.
4. Use right and left handling.
5. The previously used 'Down' command should now be introduced.
6. Leave the dog on the table while the handler progressively moves away ready to recall the dog to him.
7. Ensure that the dog can be sent ahead to get on the table and go down immediately.
8. Continue with recalls occasionally

LONG JUMP TRAINING

Many handlers approach to teaching this obstacle is based upon dragging the dog over the units. This is totally unnecessary for a more logical approach is to use just one or two units at first and with a slow increase in units and distance the dog soon learns.

INSTRUCTOR'S USE OF THE LONG JUMP AND TEACHING PROCEDURE

1. Use one or two closed up units to start with.
2. Use a recall method for first attempts.

EXPLANATION FROM INSTRUCTOR TO HANDLER

Tell the handler:-

1. To sit the dog facing the long jump unit so that he has a straight approach.
2. The lead clip should be under the dog's chin.
3. A command 'Wait' is to be given simultaneously with a flat hand signal.
4. To move to the other side of the long jump without turning their back on the dog.
5. The lead must be kept slack while moving into position.
6. Pause before calling the dog to avoid anticipation learning.
7. Use the dog's recall command, not a jump command.
8. Simultaneously call the dog and step back.
9. While stepping back smartly bring your hands, holding the lead, to the groin.
10. Praise and reward where applicable.

LIKELY PROBLEMS

Problem - The dog is stepping onto the long jump boards.
Solution - Place a low jump in front or put one element on top of the other to encourage the dog to gain height.

Problem - The dog anticipated the jump.
Solution - If temperament allows hold the dog back by the collar and also advise more work on wait control.

Problem - The dog jumped well but tipped the back element over.
Solution - None. Ignore it and try again.

TRAINING PROGRESSION WILL BE:-

1. Introduce the handler's chosen long jump command.
2. Run with the dog on the left whilst he jumps.
3. Run with the dog on the right whilst he jumps.
4. Dispense with the lead before proceeding further.
5. To run with dog being encouraged by hand signal and command to jump ahead without handler. Both handling sides should be used.
6. To run and send the dog slightly ahead to jump using a toy or tit-bit providing the dog is not too excitable. Both handling sides to be used.
7. Gradually increase long jump length as the dog gains confidence.
8. Recalling the dog over the long jump should be continued to be practised at all progression stages.
9. Introduce corner poles.

SPREAD OR PARALLEL JUMP

We strongly advise that before a dog is introduced to a spread or parallel jump that all the different stages of hurdle training have been mastered. Training for this obstacle has few problems if the dog can:-

1. Jump on command.
2. Wait until commanded to move.
3. Recall jump or be sent over.
4. Run with his handler on either side.
5. Achieve the full height jump.

The difference between these two types of double jump are self explanatory. The spread jump has two jump poles at different heights, the front pole lower than the rear pole, whilst the parallel jump has both jump poles at the same height. It is advantageous to start training with the spread jump and introduce a parallel jump as training progresses.

INSTRUCTOR'S USE OF THE SPREAD OR PARALLEL JUMP.

1. Always commence with a low narrow spread. A 15" (38 cm) high front pole with a 20" (50 cm) high rear pole set approximately 15" (38 cm) apart should suffice for most dogs. Obviously dimensions should be proportionally less for mini dogs.
2. The recall method on lead is best to start with.
3. Only increase height of poles gradually after successful attempts.
4. Introduce parallel poles whilst still at a low height.
5. Lower the poles if the dog falters and build confidence slowly.

EXPLANATION FROM INSTRUCTOR TO HANDLER

Tell the handler:-

1. All the advice given for hurdle training should apply.
2. With the dog on lead sit him facing the spread.
3. Ensure the dog is a correct distance away from the spread. This may be a little further away than for a single hurdle.
4. Your lead clip should be under the dogs chin.
5. Give the command 'Wait'.
6. Move to other side of the jump and face your dog.
7. I may assist by handing the lead to you when on the other side.
8. Use your jump command and step back as you recall your dog.
9. Praise and reward as applicable.

LIKELY PROBLEMS

Problem - The dog misjudges the jump's width and knocks down front pole.
Solution - Reduce the width for next attempt.

Problem - Dog puts his paws in between poles and/or knocks both down.
Solution - Reduce height and width for next attempt.

Problem - With the poles parallel the dog does not see the far pole and knocks it down.
Solution - Lower the front pole to just below height of rear pole.

TRAINING PROGRESSION

1. Gradually increase height of both poles simultaneously.
2. While increasing height, use parallel poles.
3. Increase width gradually and use parallel poles.
4. Alternate between recalls, running either side, and sending the dog over.

WISHING WELL OR LYCH GATE

The wishing well should never be taught to a new dog until hurdle training has been perfected, and the full height has been achieved both on single hurdles and spread jumps. The way that this obstacle is usually manufactured, the only part that can be lowered a few inches/centimetres is the jump pole. The wishing well differs from standard hurdles in three ways, all of which can have an effect on the dog as it approaches the obstacle. It has a roof, a large solid base, and is without wings. An inexperienced dog who is run at this obstacle before hurdle training has been mastered can develop faults that will be difficult to cure.

INSTRUCTOR'S USE OF THE WISHING WELL AND TEACHING PROCEDURE

1. Commence training when hurdle technique has been mastered, and the full jumping height has been achieved on single hurdles as well as spread jumps.
2. Place a hurdle wing either side of the obstacle.
3. Lower the jump pole nearer to the obstacle's base.
4. Initially use the recall method on lead.

EXPLANATION FROM INSTRUCTOR TO HANDLER

Tell the handler:-

1. All the advice given for initial hurdle training should apply.
2. Sit the dog facing the wishing well on lead.
3. Ensure the dog is a correct distance from the obstacle in relation to his size to enable him to execute the jump with ease. This should be a little further away than for a single hurdle.
4. Lead clip to be under dog's chin.
5. Give the command 'Wait'
6. Move to other side of wishing well and face your dog.
7. I may assist you at this stage by handing you the lead when you are in place on the other side.
8. Using your jump command, step back and recall your dog.
9. Praise and reward as applicable.

LIKELY PROBLEMS

Problem - Dog is nervous of the roof, or attempts to jump it.
Solution - Remove roof for initial training.

Problem - Dog runs out at wishing well.
Solution - More emphasis on command and/or use a toy in the hand as encouragement.

Problem - Dog attempts wishing well but steps on it.
Solution - Dog must not be reprimanded, only praised for the attempt. Instructor can hold another hurdle pole just above the base where the dog put his paw.

Problem - Dog knocks well pole down and steps on base.
Solution - Put hurdle in front of wishing well with pole just above the height of the base. This is to give the dog an appearance of simply jumping a hurdle.

TRAINING PROGRESSION

1. Dispense with lead.
2. Gradually increase height of wishing well jump pole.
3. Send dog over with handler static.
4. Place a hurdle in line approximately 5/6 metres from the wishing well. The dog is then to jump both obstacles with handler moving.
5. Vary the handling sides at all stages.

N.B. If a dog has been thoroughly taught the hurdle technique, at all the different stages, it may be possible to attempt the wishing well when moving with the handler by the dogs side. It is however very difficult to use the lead with this method on this obstacle and therefore the possibility of the dog making mistakes exists. Teachers must be aware of this and advise accordingly.

VIADUCT WALL

This obstacle is not too dissimilar to the wishing well, both for the dog and in its training approach. Again it should not be taught to the new dog until hurdle training has been mastered and the full height has been achieved. Apart from displaceable bricks on the top, few walls can be lowered for teaching as can be done with initial hurdle training.

THE INSTRUCTOR'S USE OF THE WALL.

1. Commence training when hurdle technique has been mastered at full height.
2. Remove displaceable bricks from the top.
3. Recall method on lead can be used initially.

EXPLANATION FROM INSTRUCTOR TO HANDLER

Tell the handler:-

1. All the advice given for initial hurdle training should apply.
2. Sit the dog facing the wall, on lead.
3. Ensure the dog is correct distance from the obstacle in relation to his size to enable him to execute the jump with ease. This should be a little further away than for a single hurdle.
4. Place lead clip under the dogs chin.
5. Give the command 'Wait'
6. Move to the other side of the wall and face the dog.
7. I may assist you on the other side of the wall by handing you the lead.
8. Using your jump command, step back and recall the dog.
9. Praise and reward as applicable.

LIKELY PROBLEMS

Problem - The dog runs around wall to handler.
Solution - Place more emphasis on jump command and/or use toy in hand as encouragement.

Problem - The dog jumps the obstacle but places paws on top.
Solution - Place a hurdle up close to the wall with jump pole just higher than the top of the wall.

TRAINING PROGRESSION

1. Dispense with lead.
2. Put displaceable bricks on wall.
3. Send the dog over with handler static.
4. Place a hurdle in line approximately 5/6 metres away from the wall. The dog is then to jump both obstacles with his handler moving.
5. Vary handling sides at all stages.

N.B. If a dog has been thoroughly taught the hurdle technique at all the different stages, it may be possible to attempt the wall from a moving position with the handler by the dog's side. It is however very difficult to use the lead with this method on this obstacle and therefore the possibility of the dog making mistakes exists. Teachers must be aware of this and advise accordingly.

WEAVING POLES

Suggested methods to use:-

1. Confined Channel Method
2. Angled Poles Method
3. Add a Pole and Incentive Method
4. Basic Method

This is the only obstacle that cannot quickly be mastered. Whereas all other obstacles have an objective that can soon be grasped by the dog this one does not. Initially a dog will always naturally want to take the shortest route to get to the end, yet on this obstacle we insist that he takes the devious route of in and out.

To achieve not only success but success with speed and style is not at all difficult providing that patience is used. It is the line of least resistance to teach the dog by pushing him in and out of the poles for it appears that he is learning quickly. This can be true but teaching by this method rarely produces a stylish freestyle weave. In many instances all the dog learns is that his handler will always be alongside and when he is not then he should stop weaving. We therefore list methods in order of preference, making a brief description of this basic method which we favour least.

The confined channel method is our preferred method and it is undoubtedly the best to use providing that it can be practised every day and not just once a week at training club. In a class situation if there are several dogs all at slightly differing standards of progress then the angled poles method is best used. The poles angles can quickly be changed to suit each level of progress whereas changing the set up with the confined channel method is not as quick.

Having written that we firmly believe that, for a handler who can be given individual attention or one who is experienced and is now contemplating training a second dog for the sport, the confined channel method is best. It is also of use for retraining dogs with weaving problems initially taught by the basic method. We therefore list it first.

WEAVING POLES

METHOD 'A' - Confined Channel.

INSTRUCTOR'S USE OF THE WEAVING POLES AND TEACHING PROCEDURE.

1. The object of teaching the confined channel method of weaving   is to teach a dog to weave fast and accurately.
2. Being able to work the dog on into the weaving poles without the necessity of his handler being beside him.
3. To be able to send the dog ahead into the poles from all angles.
4. To be able to handle on both sides.
5. No pulling or pushing is necessary with this method just good basic control.
6. If the combined channel method is to be used, either a special teaching frame and poles will be necessary or broom handles with 6" (150 mm) nails embedded.
7. In both cases galvanised wire, 3 to 4 millimetres, thick will be necessary.   When wrapped around the poles the length of the wire should be 6" (150 mm) longer than the distance between two weaving poles.

8. If the distance between poles is 21" (533 mm) twice this = 42"
    (1066 mm).   Therefore to allow the wire to curve, another 6"
    (150 mm) is necessary plus the amount to be used to wrap around
    the poles. (See illustration)
9. If a confined channel training frame is available, initially set it up so
    that the channel is approximately 18" (450 mm) wide.
10. If broom handles or similar are to be used set up the weaving poles
    in a straight line and then move every other one out 18" (450 mm)
    to make a channel. Wire is then attached to the poles on each
    side so that the channel becomes confined with just an entrance
    and exit at either end.

EXPLANATION FROM INSTRUCTOR TO HANDLER

Tell the handler:-

1. That this method must not be rushed and if short cut failure is likely.
2. That if progressively taught the confined channel method assists the
    dog never to make a mistake.
3. That the method can produce a dog who will enter the weaving poles
    ahead of his handler and from any angle with his handler on either
    side.
4. Your dog is walked through many times to accustom him to the
    channel's restriction.   He must not be allowed to jump out.
5. So that they cannot jump out the dog should be guided on a very short
    lead held almost by his collar.
6. The dog should then be recalled through the channel starting from
    a sitting position where the dog's head is passed the first pole on the
    right.
7. To send the dog through to a thrown toy or food if necessary.
8. That as an alternative such incentives can be placed rather than
    thrown. As a further initial alternative the instructor can throw
    the toy.
9. To send the dog through several times and run beside him on the
    right and left.
10. To send the dog in from several yards/metres away from the poles
    whilst remaining static, and throw the toy so that it lands ahead of
    him after he has exited.
11. To increase the angle from which the dog is sent, sometimes
    remaining static and sometimes moving towards the dog.
12. To practise angles from both sides up to at least 90 degrees.
13. That from the beginning handling will take place on randomly
    selected sides.

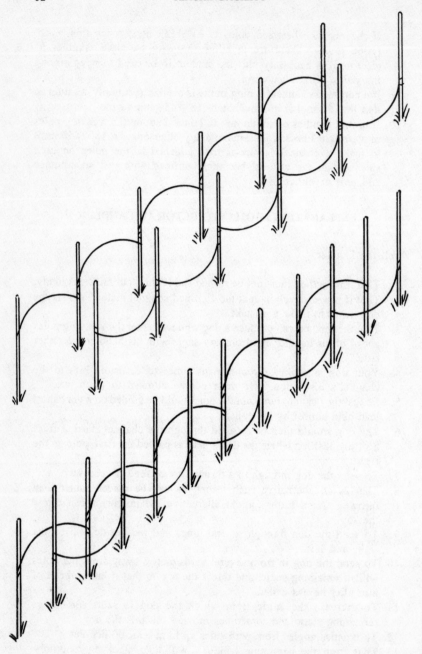

Figure 1.   Confined channel training weave

LIKELY PROBLEMS:-

Problem - Initially some dogs will attempt to jump over or duck under the wires.

Solution - The dog should be guided through on a shorter lead.

Problem - The timing of the thrown toy, its trajectory and direction, is a distraction, or is sometimes unseen by the dog.

Solution - In such cases the instructor or an assistant should be the thrower.

Problem - The dog appears to be getting bored.

Solution - Shorter sessions should be advised.

TRAINING PROGRESSION WILL BE:-

1. To introduce the chosen weaving command.
2. To gradually decrease channel width but leave the entrance and exit slightly less decreased until there is no longer a channel.
3. After every initial channel reduction the dog should be walked through several times to ensure that he does not try and jump out.
4. Add a hurdle at the far end so that the dog learns to work on after exiting the poles.
5. Continue training by handling in every possible position.
6. Progressively remove one wire each side starting at the middle.
7. Practise from every position as before without any wires from every previously trained position.
8. If the dog goes wrong twice consecutively revert to a previous stage.
9. The dog should be practised on odd and even numbers of poles.

WEAVING POLES

METHOD 'B' - Angled poles

This method is similar to the one previously described in that it creates a natural path for the dog to follow. It allows for him to be taught to work without his handler being alongside and to be taught by play or food motivation.

INSTRUCTOR'S USE OF THE WEAVING POLES AND TEACHING PROCEDURE

1. The object of teaching the angled poles method of weaving is to teach a dog to weave fast and accurately.
2. To work weaving poles without the necessity of his handler being beside him.

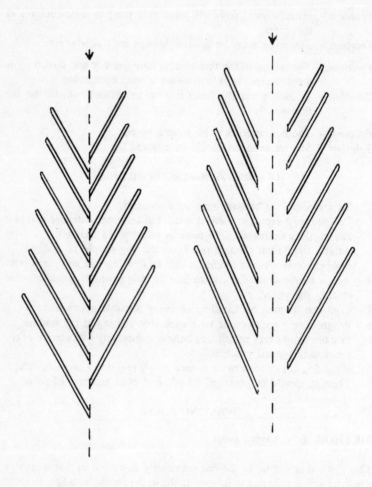

Initially the poles can be angled from a straight line or
with a gap between to create a more defined path. The
angle of the poles can also be increased beyond that
shown here.

Figure 2. Angled weaving poles

3. To be able to handle on both sides.
4. No pulling or pushing is necessary, just good basic control.
5. Use broom handles just a fraction taller than the head of the largest dogs under training. Poles that are too high will be an encumbrance when first walking the dog through by lead.
6. Set up twelve weaving poles approximately 20" (508 mm) apart. First create a gap of approximately 6" (150 mm) by staggering the poles in a similar way to that described for the previous method. Angle the first pole to the left and the second to the right, and then alternate the bend of all poles until the end is reached. The angle that the poles are initially set at should be considerable, leaving a wide definite natural path through the middle.

EXPLANATION FROM INSTRUCTOR TO HANDLER

Tell the handler:-

1. That this method must not be rushed and if short cut failure is most likely to occur.
2. The dog(s) are walked through many times to accustom them to the natural path. They must not be allowed to jump out.
3. The dog should be guided on a short lead through the natural path several times to ensure that he is familiar with the route he will be expected to take.
4. If the dog is reluctant to enter the natural path or is struggling to get out then reduce the number of poles considerably to make the set up look less imposing for the dog.
5. The dog should then be recalled through the natural path several times.
6. Next place an incentive at the far end. This can be food or a toy. With some dogs the instructor strategically placed at the end can throw a ball to encourage the dog to run through on his own. Repeat this stage several times.
7. Now the dog should be sent through the poles while the handler runs alongside. Both handling sides should be used from the beginning and should be alternated randomly.
8. As the dog progresses and with the right type of dog the handler should attempt to let him work on ahead into the poles.
9. Once the dog starts to really understand his handler's requirements then the handler can throw a toy ahead of him as he exits.
10. That from the beginning handling will take place on randomly selected sides.

LIKELY PROBLEMS:-

Problem - The dog will leave the natural path prematurely.
Solution - Progress is being attempted too quickly. Revert to an earlier
            stage. The dog should be guided through on a shorter lead.
Problem - The timing of the thrown toy, its trajectory and direction, is
            a distraction, or is sometimes unseen by the dog.
Solution - The instructor or an assistant should be the thrower.
Problem - The dog appears to be getting bored.
Solution - Shorter sessions should be advised.

TRAINING PROGRESSION WILL BE:-

1. Introduce the chosen weave command.
2. Over a period of time, which may be weeks, gradually reduce the
    6"(150 mm) gap to zero and gradually move the poles to an
    upright position.
3. As the poles are gradually moved upright leave the entrance and exit
    poles less upright than the others.
4. Add a hurdle at the far end so that the dog learns to work on after
    exiting the poles.
5. Continue training by handling in every possible position.
6. If the dog goes wrong twice consecutively revert to a previous stage.
7. The dog should be practised on odd and even numbers of poles.

WEAVING POLES

METHOD 'C' Add a pole and incentive

INSTRUCTOR'S USE OF THE WEAVING POLES AND TEACHING PROCEDURE.

1. The object of teaching the add a pole and incentive method is to
    teach a dog to weave fast and accurately.
2. To be able to handle on both sides.
3. No pulling or pushing is necessary just enthusiasm to chase a toy or
    tug.
4. Broom handles with 6" (150 mm) embedded in the bottom are best
    for this method.
5. Two poles approximately 20" (508) apart should initially be placed
    upright in the ground.
6. The dog should not be on a lead for this method. If the dogs attention
    cannot be kept unless confined on a lead then this is not a suitable
    method.

EXPLANATION FROM INSTRUCTOR TO HANDLER

Tell the handler:-

1. The dog should be off lead.
2. That this method relies on good timing of any toy used as a lure.
3. That initially with his dog on the left the lure will be held   in the right hand.
4. That when his dog is being handled on the right the lure will be held in the left hand.
5. That the lure should always be kept 6" (150 mm) from the dog's nose and moved progressively through the gaps as he is teased to get to it.
6. That at the end he will be allowed to catch it and a game of tug or play retrieve will follow.
7. That poles will be added as the dog progresses.
8. That from the beginning handling will take place on randomly selected sides.

LIKELY PROBLEMS:-

Problem - The dog will catch the lure too soon.
Solution - Better control of the lure is required.

Problem - The dog loses interest in the lure.
Solution - This is the wrong method for such a dog.

Problem - The dog will only chase the lure when the handler is on a certain side.
Solution - Insufficient practise has been carried out on one side. Revert to an applicable point in training and for a while the dog should only be practised on the side he has been having difficulty with.

TRAINING PROGRESSION WILL BE:-

1. To introduce the chosen weaving command.
2. To gradually add further poles.
3. To add a hurdle at the far end so that the dog learns to work on after exiting the poles.
4. Training will be continued by handling the dog on both left and right.
5. If the dog goes wrong twice consecutively revert to a previous training stage .
6. The dog should be practised on odd and even numbers of poles.

WEAVING POLES

METHOD 'D' - Basic method

INSTRUCTOR'S USE OF WEAVING POLES AND
TEACHING PROCEDURE

1. This method is simple to teach and explain and relatively quick for the dog to learn. It does however have disadvantages for many dogs taught by this method.
2. Twelve poles approximately 20" (508 mm) apart should be placed upright in the ground, or weave poles on a frame should be used.
3. The length of the poles should be such that they will pass under the handler's armpit.

EXPLANATION FROM INSTRUCTOR TO HANDLER

Tell the handler:-

1. That this method relies on repetition and guiding the dog by lead through the poles.
2. That with his dog on the left he should be guided through the first opening and back out through the second.
3. That this system is used until the dog reaches the end.
4. That one command can be used as the dog commences or commands 'In' and 'Out' should be used where applicable.
5. That from the beginning handling will take place on randomly selected sides.

LIKELY PROBLEMS:-

Problem - The dog will not easily be guided.
Solution - Use another method.

Problem - The dog resents the use of the lead.
Solution - Use another method.

Problem - The dog takes a long time to learn.
Solution - Use another method.

Problem - The dog will not start to weave unless the handler is with him.
Solution - Use another method.

TRAINING PROGRESSION WILL BE:-

1. To remove the lead but, as a transition, continue making all the same movements and signals that the lead arm has previously made.
2. To try and speed the dog through.
3. To add a hurdle at the far end so that the dog learns to work on after exiting the poles.
4. Training will be continued by handling the dog on both left and right.
5. If the dog goes wrong twice consecutively revert to a previous stage.
6. The dog should be practised on odd and even numbers of poles.

GENERAL WEAVING ADVICE

No matter what methods are to be used to teach the dog, handlers should be advised to take every opportunity to practise on other sets of weaving poles at other venues. If not, a dog with a perfect weave at home, or in class, will probably look at the first different weave he encounters in competition with a complete lack of understanding. In other words he will only have been trained to weave in one or two venues at the most and not yet with poles at any venue. However until proficient at class or home other people's weaving poles should not be attempted.

Once the dog has become a proficient weaver then the handler must be advised to practise with odd and even numbers of poles. If an even number is always used then the dog will always exit to his left. That is now his habit and he may be confused when an odd number of poles are used and he will be expected to exit to the right.

As well as odds and evens, 5 to 13 poles should be practised. Although that extra pole may be illegal in competition, it does help to teach the dog to continue weaving if the pole is there rather than rely on the rhythm of the eleven movements he must make when there are 12 poles.

An instructors ultimate aim must be to produce a partnership where the dog is able to weave correctly at speed and without hesitation. Therefore, during early training or competition, it is imperative that the dog is not scolded for making a mistake. For the sake of long term weaving accuracy it is preferable to tell handlers to ignore mistakes and, where applicable, start from the beginning again. In such circumstances the handler must be made aware that the dog is unwittingly likely to repeat his same error and therefore they should consider extra vocal assistance at the previous point of error. We do not advise a handler tries to restart his dog at the point of error either in training or competition.

'A' RAMP

This imposing obstacle is, in reality, one of the easiest for the dog to learn to negotiate. Once a dog has started to learn other obstacles all he needs to be made aware of is, that once he reaches the top, there is a way down. Unfortunately walking him round the other side to show it to him does not achieve this. It will be found that once the dog has been over this obstacle once or twice he is quite happy to tackle it without resistance. Having instructed hundreds of dogs of different breeds to negotiate this obstacle in the way we describe below we have found it totally unnecessary to lower the 'A' ramp for teaching purposes.

INSTRUCTOR'S USE OF THE 'A' RAMP AND TEACHING PROCEDURE

1. The 'A' ramp is the first contact obstacle to be taught.
2. We recommend three possible methods shown as 'A', 'B', and 'C'.
3. For method 'A' the handler and instructor will be on opposite sides of the dog and Ramp so that at all times the instructor can see what is happening.
4. For method 'B' the instructor will handle the dog.
5. With method 'C' the instructor will handle the dog over the apex.

METHOD 'A' - Handler running the dog up

EXPLANATION FROM INSTRUCTOR TO HANDLER

Tell the handler:-

1. To make a straight approach to the obstacle with his dog from 2/3 yards/metres away.
2. That the lead should be held just above the dog's head with an underhand grip by the hand nearest the dog.
3. That two thirds of the way up is the critical point where the dog is likely to come off the side towards his handler.
4. The handler and instructor should not get ahead of the dog, but stay approximately in line with his shoulders.
5. As the dog gets near the apex the handler should extend his nearest arm to the dog to achieve a locked position but retain control with a short lead.
6. The instructor and handler should position themselves close to the bottom of the up side, leaving no room for the dog to squeeze past them.
7. Throughout the attempt the instructor will be in a position to give assistance to the dog, either physical, verbal or both.
8. A toy or tit-bit should be used as encouragement if necessary.

9. On the down side the dog must touch at least two thirds of the contact. Handlers should be advised about the safety importance of contacts.
10. The dog and handler should proceed in a straight line away from the obstacle when completed.
11. Praise and reward if applicable.

LIKELY PROBLEMS:-

Problem - The dog struggles and comes back down the obstacle ?
Solution - Make another attempt, give more assistance,

Problem - The dog will not go up after several attempts ?
Solution - Use a different method such as method 'B' or 'C' below.

Problem - The dog came off the side, handler is too short ?
Solution - Instructor on table to take lead from handler.

TRAINING PROGRESSION WILL BE:-

1. The handler with the dog still on lead should continue attempts without the instructor's assistance.
2. Introduce the handler's chosen command for the obstacle.
3. The lead should be dispensed with as soon as possible.
4. Introduce right and left handling as soon as possible.
5. If hoops are to be used to encourage confidence and speed over the obstacle without missing contacts they should be introduced now. (See Chapter 4 - 'Contact Methods')
6. A contact method should now be established.

METHOD 'B' - Handler on the far side of the ramp

EXPLANATION FROM INSTRUCTOR TO HANDLER

Tell the handler:-

1. To climb up the far side of the 'A' ramp.
2. They must position themselves to one side of the 'A' ramp apex to allow the dog to pass.
3. The instructor will handle the lead as in method 'A'.
4. When told to do so they should encourage the dog up with the use of a toy or food if necessary.
5. When the dog reaches the apex the instructor will work the dog down the far side without interference from his handler.
6. They should remain in position for further attempts.
7. Several successful attempts should be made before reverting to method 'A'.

TRAINING PROGRESSION

The training progression will be as that described in Method 'A'

METHOD 'C' - Instructor standing on the table

EXPLANATION FROM INSTRUCTOR TO HANDLER

Tell the handler:-

1. To place an agility table adjacent to the 'A' ramp in line with the apex.   If possible slide at least half of the table underneath the 'A' Ramp so that there is minimum obstruction for the handler to pass.
2. That the instructor will stand on the table.
3. That the handler should work the dog as described in method 'A'.
4. That as the dog reaches approximately two thirds of the way up the ramp you will take the lead and handle the dog over the apex.
5. That as soon as the instructor has the lead the handler should go to the far side of the ramp to encourage the dog to come down and take the lead to control the decent.
6. Several such attempts should be made if necessary.

TRAINING PROGRESSION

The training progression will be as described in Method 'A'

DOG WALK

This is another obstacle that looks difficult for beginners and also one that is not necessary to lower. Again the dog's only real difficulty is not knowing there is a way out. Whereas with the 'A' ramp he has the easy possibility of returning down the way he went up, with this obstacle's narrow planks his initial concern is likely to be greater.   The main objective is to instil confidence that he can negotiate the obstacle.

INSTRUCTOR'S USE OF THE DOG WALK AND TEACHING PROCEDURE

1. The dog walk is the second contact obstacle to be taught, and is always taught before the see-saw.
2. The handler and instructor should be on opposite sides of the dog and the first plank when it is reached.
3. Throughout initial attempts the instructor must always be in a position close to the dog to immediately assist and to inhibit any attempts the dog may make to alight.

METHOD 'A' - Walking the dog up

EXPLANATION FROM INSTRUCTOR TO HANDLER

Tell the handler:-

1. We will see if the dog will go up the dog walk without a problem.
2. I will help you by being on the other side of the dog.
3. We will both make a straight on approach commencing at about 2/3 yards/metres from the bottom of the up side.
4. The lead should be held in the hand nearest the dog.
5. Should your dog struggle, either I or both of us will hold the dogs collar for greater control.
6. On approach the dog will be close between us. When we reach the plank we must both be close to the sides of the planks with the dog still between us leaving him no room to squeeze past.
7. We must not get ahead of the dog. In line with his shoulders is the best position.
8. We will lead the dog up without fuss or excitement and use as much encouragement as necessary.
9. If you think it will help use a toy or tit-bit to encourage your dog.
10. On the down side at least two thirds of the contact should be walked on by the dog before allowing him to get off.
11. We will then proceed in a straight line away from the obstacle.
12. Praise and reward if applicable.

LIKELY PROBLEMS:-

Problem - The dog gets between handler and obstacle and the attempt fails ?

Solution - The instructor must advise why this has happened and ensure they are both close to the plank on the next attempt.

Problem - After two attempts it is clear that the dog's lack of confidence and struggles make this method unsuitable.

Solution - Use an alternative method of placing the dog on the top plank at the descent end of that plank to show him there is a way out (see Method 'B'). Use the table if necessary to make lifting the dog easier.

Problem - The dog is nervous of the instructor and objects to being crowded by a stranger ?

Solution - Ask the handler to use someone the dog is familiar with to assist while the instructor supervises.

TRAINING PROGRESSION

1. The handler with the dog still on lead should attempt without instructor's assistance.
2. Introduce the handler's chosen command for the obstacle.
3. The lead should be dispensed with as soon as possible.
4. Introduce right and left handling as soon as possible.
5. If hoops are to be used to encourage confidence and speed over the obstacle without missing contacts, they should be introduced now (see Chapter 4 'Contact Methods'). If method 'C' has been used the dog may have already been introduced to hoops.
6. A contact method should now be established.

METHOD 'B' - Allowing the dog to see the way out

EXPLANATION FROM INSTRUCTOR TO HANDLER

1. Lift the dog on to the top plank at the descent end and if necessary, use the table to do so.
2. We will both stay close to the dog on either side of the plank. This position should be approximately level with his shoulder.
3. We will hold his collar with the nearest hand to him leaving the other hand free for encouragement.
4. Before moving him down, calm and soothe him.
5. Lead him down with encouragement.
6. If you think it will help use a toy or tit-bit to encourage your dog.
7. On the down side at least two thirds of the contact should be walked on by the dog before allowing him to get off.
8. We will then proceed in a straight line away from the obstacle.
9. Praise and reward if applicable.

LIKELY PROBLEMS:-

Problem - The dog fell off the plank and the attempt fails ?
Solution - The instructor must advise why this has happened and ensure they are both close to the plank on the next attempt.

Problem - After two attempts it is clear that the dogs lack of confidence and struggles make this method unsuitable.
Solution - Use an alternative method such as a training plank (See method 'C')

Problem - The dog is nervous of the instructor and objects to being crowded by a stranger and there is no one familiar with the dog to assist?
Solution - Use method 'C' while the instructor supervises.

TRAINING PROGRESSION

1. Continue lifting the dog onto the top plank at the descent end until he is confident.
2. After each successful attempt continue placing the dog further back along the top plank.
3. When the dog is confident from the ascent end of the top plank proceed as for method 'A'.

METHOD 'C' - Training plank with wire mesh

This is best used by experienced handlers bringing on a new dog. It allows dogs to learn to run quickly over the planks without any apprehension. It also has a use for a very difficult dog with a beginner handler.

As the method is taught by motivation rather than compulsion, if well taught the result is a dog who will run at speed over the obstacle. However it is almost essential to use hoops in conjunction with this method to ensure that the dog's speed to get to whatever is being used to motivate him does not result in him learning to jump prematurely off the bottom of the plank. Doing so would of course be the first lessons in missing contacts. (For hoops see Chapter 4 'Contact Methods')

Equipment:-

A twelve foot scaffold plank and an Agility table or a natural bank to rest the plank on are required. Staple rigid wire mesh approximately 12" (30 cm) high onto the sides of the plank. Rest the plank on the edge of the table or a grass bank. Ensure that a toy or tit-bit is available to use as motivation.

EXPLANATION FROM INSTRUCTOR TO HANDLER

1. Call the dog onto the table or bank.
2. Use a toy or tit-bit to encourage him down.
3. When he is happy at descending encourage him to walk up as well.
4. If a hoop is to be used introduce one now at the bottom of the plank.
5. When confident going up and down revert to dog walk method 'A' continuing to use motivation and hoops at this stage.

TRAINING PROGRESSION

The training progression will be as described in Method 'A'

SEE-SAW

This obstacle is no more than a dog walk that moves, therefore teaching it should always be after mastery of the dog walk. Dogs natural dislike of things that move under their feet is really the only difference and, as with all contact obstacle training, it is all about instilling confidence in the dog.

INSTRUCTOR'S USE OF THE SEE-SAW AND TEACHING PROCEDURE

1. See-saw training commences after the dog-walk has been mastered.
2. The handler and instructor will be on opposite sides of the dog and plank so that at all times the instructor can see what is happening.

EXPLANATION FROM INSTRUCTOR TO HANDLER

Tell the handler:-

1. He should have the dog on one side and that you will be on the other.
2. The dog is to be held on a very short lead by both of us using the hands nearest to the dog.
3. We will make a straight on approach commencing about 2/3 yards or metres from the bottom of the up side.
4. Should your dog struggle, either I or both of us will hold the dog's collar for greater control.
5. On approach the dog will be close between us. When we reach the plank we must both be close to the sides of the planks with the dog still between us leaving him no room to squeeze past.
6. We must not get ahead of the dog. In line with his shoulders is the best position.
7. We will lead the dog up without fuss or excitement and use as much encouragement as necessary.
8. If you think it will help use a toy or tit-bit to encourage your dog by keeping it just ahead of him.
9. The dog must be stopped to learn to pause but not before reaching the tipping point.
10. If necessary an assistant can control the planks tip from behind.
11. If there is no assistant to help the instructor must take the tipping weight at the appropriate time using his free hand.
12. On the down side at least two thirds of the contact should be walked on by the dog before allowing him to get off.
13. We will then proceed in a straight line away from the obstacle rather than turning back immediately for another attempt.
14. Praise and reward if applicable.

LIKELY PROBLEMS:-

Problem - The dog struggles and succeeds in walking beside the plank?
Solution - The handler and instructor must ensure this does not happen again.
Problem - The dog is nervous of the instructor and objects to being crowded by a stranger ?
Solution - Ask handler to get someone the dog is familiar with to assist while the instructor supervises.

TRAINING PROGRESSION WILL BE:-

1. The handler with the dog still on lead should attempt without instructor's assistance.
2. Introduce the handler's chosen command for the obstacle.
3. Introduce the handler's pause command.
4. Lead should be dispensed with as soon as possible.
5. Introduce right and left handling as soon as possible.
6. If hoops are to be used to encourage confidence and speed over the obstacle without missing contacts, they should be introduced now, (see Chapter 4. 'Contact Obstacle Methods'.)
7. A contact method should now be established.

4

Contact Methods

As this subject is so important we have deliberately left it as a separate chapter although it should be read in conjunction with any contact obstacles being taught. This is the facet of Agility that is most difficult to achieve consistent success with. Many dogs will start off making their contacts in training and competition then, as the excitement and anticipation level increases, they start to miss them. This is inevitable if no definite method of keeping the dog on contacts has been established. Unfortunately it also applies to some dogs who have been taught a method which previously was successful. Many dogs will need to have their method changed during their Agility career, and instructors must know all the best methods so advice can be given when necessary.

Initially an instructor should advise a certain method which is to be used for all three contact obstacles. Needless to say that method should be consistently and properly applied for some considerable time before the handler is allowed to discard it. All methods require a lot of practise to establish the habit for that is how dogs learn what we require. It is just a question of consistency.

Before teaching any new handler it is as well to understand why a dog will miss contacts. The answer is quite simple in that we are constantly striving for speed over obstacles and course. Speed and running to the end of planks are opposites when the dog can see a quicker way by departing earlier than we would wish. Agility speed is also all about the dog anticipating the next obstacle to be negotiated, and there is nothing like anticipation for teaching a dog to miss out a part of the exercise.

Instructors must carefully advise their pupils and ensure that contacts are never missed in training so that positive training is undertaken rather than negative misses or near misses of contacts. For this reason we advise that during most training sessions the contact method is employed each time the dog negotiates an applicable obstacle.

Summary:-

1. If well taught most dogs start their competition career by running over contacts points.
2. Without a definite method of conveying to the dog that he must not alight at any point that he wishes to, as he gains in confidence, he is likely to start prematurely leaving the obstacle.
3. Body language problems must be pointed out at this stage to ensure that the dog is not getting an incorrect message. A handler's slightest premature movement away from the obstacle can convey such a message to their dog who will see this movement as instructions to leave.
4. When training, a handler that is consistently satisfied with their dog covering just a few inches or centimetres of contact before alighting will invariably find that the dog will miss contacts by a considerable amount in competition.
5. Instructors must be aware that some commands given by handlers supposedly to keep the dog on the contact, can be construed by the dog as commands to get off. For example a handler who gives three 'Wait' commands as the dog slowly descends but consistently uses the wrong body language by moving off in conjunction with the third 'Wait' will teach the dog that the third 'Wait' means alight.
6. Try and ensure that the dog is not crowded by his handler which in some instances will cause the dog to jump off the side.

METHODS

HOOPS

Used for speed and the transition to a method.

1. An instructor's aim must be to teach a handler to train their dog to rocket over contact obstacles yet make the contacts at both ends. Hoops allow for speed and a method to be established.
2. Speed and the contacts are, to a certain extent, opposites for speed over the obstacles naturally conveys to him "Get to the next obstacle as quick as possible".

3. Hoops can be used to cover the transitional period of teaching speed without needing to teach contact accuracy at such a stage. They enable the handler to train for maximum speed without using any negative vocal or physical reinforcement to stop the dog jumping off too soon.

4. You must make it quite clear to your pupils that hoops alone will not ensure that a dog never misses a contact. All they achieve is to ensure that the dog does not learn bad habits of jumping off too soon while speed and a contact method are being established.

MAKING HOOPS

1. Plastic tubing, such as used for underground water pipes, is ideal for making hoops. For a collie sized dog a length of 1.8 metres is enough. For larger breeds the length will need to be increased up to 2 metres.

2. Both ends should be joined together to form a hoop and this is easily done by using a length of wooden dowel approximately 8" (200 mm) in length that fits reasonably tight inside the tubing.

3. A 6" (150 mm) nail through the tube allows the hoop to be secured to the ground, but to avoid splitting the wooden dowel it is best to first drill a pilot hole slightly smaller than the diameter of the nail.

USING HOOPS

1. Most dogs must be taught the use of hoops before being introduced to them in conjunction with contacts. If the dog will play, his favourite toy strategically held at the opening's far side will tempt him through hoops on the first occasions. If not use food.

2. The dog will not be ready to accept hoops at the end of contacts until sufficient training has been accomplished so that it is natural for the dog to pass through them.

3. The hoops need to be placed within a hands width of where each plank touches the ground. If necessary hoops larger than the dog under training can be tilted in such a way that the effect is to make the aperture smaller. Placed correctly it becomes impossible for the dog trained to use them, to do anything other than run all the way up from the base and all the way down to the bottom of the other side. In such a way a habit of doing just this is being formed rather than any risk of an undesirable habit of missing the contact developing.

4. Place hoops at each end of the contact and initially the dog must continue to be motivated with toy or food to pass through and be praised as he does so. He must not be expected to pass through as he did when the hoop was away from the contact. He now must be re-taught to go through the hoop at the end of the contact obstacle.

5. On the up side consistent use of a hoop will certainly teach a dog not to start his climb too high up, and avoids the alternative of a 'Down' command right at the bottom.   What we are aiming for is a quick approach and fluid traversal of the obstacle and in this context to put the dog in a 'Down' is counter productive.

6. Once speed over the contacts and through the hoops has been established, a definite method of teaching the dog to stay on the contact can be commenced.

HEEL CONTACT METHOD

1. This method is often carried out in the heel position and relies on the dog already being totally and immediately responsive to the command 'Heel'. If the handler's heel work control is not total then this is not an advisable method.

2. It should of course be taught with the dog handled on the right side as well, and an alternative command may be substituted for 'Heel' on both sides once the dog knows what is expected.

FOOD CONTACT METHOD 1

1. This method relies on a greedy dog, and the dog's most favourite small tit-bits should be used.

2. The handler should be sideways on to the dog with the tit-bit secreted in the hand furthest away from the dog.

3. As the dog descends the right hand is brought across the body and held almost at the bottom centre of the contact area.

4. The idea is that the dog is enticed to run all the way down the contact to reach the food. When he reaches it he should be allowed to have it without his momentum being stopped.

5. In training, whilst the hand should always make the same enticing movement, food should only be in it on approximately three descents out of five.

6. Exactly the same movements are used in competition so that the dog is enticed towards the hand but, of course, as nothing can be held in the hand on these occasions the dog will not be fed.

7. Both handling sides should be used and practised from the beginning.

FOOD CONTACT METHOD 2

1. As discussed above this method relies on a greedy dog, and the dog's most favourite tit-bits should be used.

2. The handler should be sideways on to the dog with the tit-bit secreted in the hand furthest away from the dog.

3. As the dog descends the right hand is brought across the body and offered to the dog as he descends from the top but before he reaches the contact. As his nose gets to approximately 10" (254 mm) in front of the tit-bit the hand should be drawn down the contact maintaining the distance between nose and hand.
4. The idea is that the dog is enticed to run all the way down the contact to reach the food but before the bottom is reached the dog is allowed to catch up with the hand. When he reaches it he should be given the food while his momentum is maintained.
5. In training whilst the hand will always make the same enticing movement food should only be in it on approximately three descents out of five.
6. Exactly the same movements are used in competition so that the dog is enticed towards the hand but, of course, as nothing can be held in the hand on these occasions the dog will not be fed.
7. Both handling sides should be used and practised from the beginning.

TOY METHOD. 1.

1. This method relies upon a dog with a good retrieve instinct and assumes that the handler has taught his dog to play.
2. The choice of the toy to be used can be critical. A ball is ideal for if thrown it will normally go where it is intended, and is small enough for the handler to carry in a pocket when not required.
3. The handler should be sideways on to the dog with the toy in the hand furthest away from the dog.
4. As the dog descends down the obstacle, but before he reaches the contact, the handler should gain his attention on the toy and lure him down to the bottom of the contact. At this point the dog should be allowed to have the toy.
5. The idea is much the same as the way we described with food whereby the dog is enticed all the way down a contact for a favourite toy.
6. If used in conjunction with hoops the toy can be tossed through the hoop at the last second to encourage the dog to pass through it to reach his reward.
7. In competition the same hand movements should be employed but, of course, there will not be a toy present.

TOY METHOD 2.

1. Again this method assumes the dog will retrieve and play.
2. The handler should place the toy on the ground a hands width away from the bottom of the contact.
3. The dog can now be sent over the obstacle to retrieve the toy.

4.   If used in conjunction with hoops, the toy must be placed the correct distance away from the hoop. This distance will depend on the size of the dog and is to ensure that the dog must pass through the hoop in order to retrieve his toy. In so doing he must run down all of the contact area.
5.   This method may be best used where a handler is not quick enough to get to the other side of a contact obstacle to use hand signals, food, or any kind of lure.
6.   In order to reinforce the dog's actions whilst descending the contact for the toy, a command such as: 'Find it', 'Where is it', 'Ball' or 'Toy' can be used, and of course it can also be used in competition.

HOLDING METHOD.

1.   The handler should be sideways on to the dog.
2.   As the dog descends the hand nearest him is brought up in front of his nose, over the top of his head, and then is pressed down on to his neck to hold him on the contact.
3.   When he is on the bottom part of the contact the hand is brought up and his momentum allowed to continue.
4.   In training, whilst the same movements will always be made to establish the signal, the hand should only press down on the dog's neck on approximately three out of five descents.
5.   In competition exactly the same movements are made, as the dog should, after constant training repetition, know exactly what the signal means. The one big difference is that the hand should not be pressed down on to his neck as touching the dog is faulted. Sufficient daylight should be left between hand and neck so that the judge can see that the handler has not touched the dog.
6.   Both handling sides should be used and practised from the beginning.

DOWN CONTACT METHOD 1.

1.   This method relies on creating an extra part of the exercise. If the exercise is regularly extended, with a down at the end, dogs, being creatures of habit, will not be so likely to anticipate the next obstacle until they have completed this final part of the exercise.
2.   An immediate response to the command 'Down' is necessary for this method to be successful.
3.   The handler should be sideways on to the dog and the 'Down' command should be given as the dog reaches the last part of the contact so that he is downed on the contact itself. Not all dogs are capable of going down on the 'A' Ramp but none should have trouble on the other two contact obstacles.

4. If the dog under training cannot down on the 'A' ramp contact then the following variation of this method can be used whilst "method 1" is retained for the other two contacts. (See Down contact method 2)

5. As an additional incentive during training a tit-bit can often be fed to the dog once he is down.

6. A signal and/or command should be developed with this method so that the dog who will not be downed in competition still expects that final command to be given.

7. Both handling sides should be used and practised from the beginning.

DOWN CONTACT METHOD 2.

1. This method relies on creating an extra part of the exercise. If the exercise is regularly extended, with a down at the end, dogs, being creatures of habit, will not be so likely to anticipate the next obstacle until they have completed this final part of the exercise.

2. An immediate response to the command 'Down' is necessary for this method to be successful.

3. The handler should be sideways on to the dog and the 'Down' command should be given as the dog leaves the contact so that he must down as close to the contact as possible. The consistency of this down extremely close to the contact is the secret of success. An almost imaginary line must be drawn past which the dog should not be allowed to go down. To go into a down so close to the bottom the dog cannot prematurely jump off.

4. As an additional incentive during training a tit-bit can often be fed to the dog once he is down.

5. A signal and/or command should be developed with this method so that the dog who should not be downed in competition still expects that final command to be given.

6. Both handling sides should be used and practised from the beginning.

1. Ready for first hurdle lessons.

2. Dog jumps - handler steps back.

3. For the table the instructor handles.

4. A second method of table teaching.

5. A table teaching method for the most reluctant.

6. Early hoop (tyre) lessons.

7. Teach the long jump by recalling over one unit.

8. How to teach a dog to gain height on a long jump.

9. Walking a learner dog up the dog walk.

10. Lifting up the more difficult dog.

11. Running a learner dog up the 'A' ramp.

12. An 'A' ramp method for shorter handlers.

13. The 'A' ramp recall method rarely fails.

14. Instructor leads dog down after recall method.

15. The correct initial see-saw approach.

16. Steadying the dog for the tilt.

17. The instructor controls the plank weight.

18. Waking and encouraging the dog to the bottom.

19. Dog running through angled weave poles for his toy.

20. The angles of the poles are progressively lessened.

21. Sending the dog through the wired channel for his toy.

22. The dog has learned a confident weave.

23. John and Peter supervise initial tunnel lessons.

24. A mini Cavalier learns by recall.

25. An easy way to teach the collapsible tunnel.

26. John holds the folded cloth. Peter handles.

27. Using food for contacts.

28. Teaching the hoop prior to its use with contacts.

29. The hoop, contact and toy.

30. An immediate down for contact training.

31. Teaching the dog to turn right -'This way'

32. Box training. An essential control exercise.

5

The Basis of Free Style Handling

WORKING WITH 3 HURDLES

Now that your students have mastered all the obstacles they will be almost ready to commence obstacle sequences, but not quite. Before they are let loose on this prerequisite of running complete courses you should ensure that they are achieving maximum speed combined with control in basic situations. They should have already been started along this road by teaching their dog that they will pass either side while he negotiates number an obstacle. To achieve the basis of free style handling we advise that three hurdles are used in various combinations. So much can be taught with just three hurdles which will prepare your students for later sequencing using the other obstacles as well. Each combination will have specific purposes.

RECALL JUMPING

Set up three hurdles in a straight line with approximately 6 yards (5.5 metres) in between each one.

1. Ask your handler to recall their dog over hurdle number 1 just as they did when originally teaching the hurdle, but lead free.
2. Stage one should have been successful and if so ask the handler to repeat the exercise but this time they should stand as close to the face of the second hurdle as possible.
3. With the dog left in a 'Wait' in front of hurdle number 1 the handler should now be positioned close to the far side of hurdle number 2

Key D = Dog H = Handler

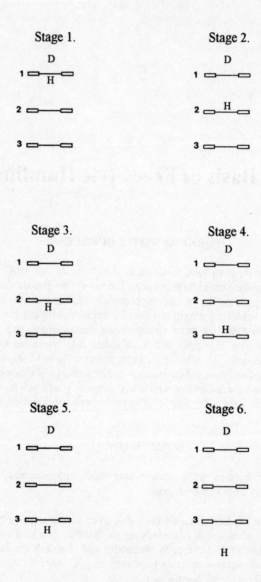

Figure 3. Recall jumping

so that his hands can encourage the dog over. As the dog is called over the first hurdle he should be encouraged over the second by the handler extending his arms over it using them as a signal while moving back as the dog jumps. This should be repeated several times before proceeding further.

4. If the foregoing has been successful ask the handler to repeat the exercise but this time they should stand as close to the face of the third hurdle as possible.

5. With the handler standing at the far side of hurdle number 3 the dog should be called over the first and second hurdles and be encouraged over the third hurdle by the handler extending his arms over it and using them as a signal while moving back as the dog jumps. This should be repeated several times before proceeding further.

6. If all previous stages have been successful ask the handler to repeat the exercise but he should stand further away from hurdle number 3.

Important:

As each of these recall jumps are successful praise and enthusiasm should be used as the dog joins the handler. If the dog will not wait at the start the Instructor should advise that more work should be carried out on this facet of training at home and at other places away from the agility area.

Summary:-

1. Recall over hurdle 1
2. Repeat 1 but with handler standing close to the second hurdle.
3. Recall over hurdles 1 and 2
4. Repeat 3 but with handler standing close to the third hurdle.
5. Recall over all three hurdles.
6. Repeat five but with handler standing further away from the third hurdle.

★   ★   ★

WORKING ON

Much more difficult for some is teaching their dog to work on ahead without constantly looking back. There is a danger of a dog that has this habit of looking back learning to circle if his handler has not caught up.

Once again three hurdles in a straight line are used for this exercise. If, as recommended in the early parts of the chapter the dog under training has been taught to play then it is simple to teach 'Working On'. If not food can be used, but first the dog must learn to key to a food container so that when he fully understands where the food comes from that container can be thrown to motivate him to go to it. Obviously when he does reach it he should be fed a morsel from it. An ideal air tight container for this use is a 35 mm plastic film container.

1.   Send over hurdle 1.

Ask the handler to send the dog over hurdle number 1 just ahead of him and as he rises over the jump instruct him to throw the object so that it lands just in front of the second hurdle. A simultaneous command and signal should be given. If the dog has picked up the object he should be called back but not over the hurdle. If not the handler must retrieve the object himself. This exercise should be repeated two or three times.

2.   Send over hurdle 2.

Now place the handler in front of the landing side of the first hurdle so that he has his back to it. Instruct the handler to run with his dog towards the second hurdle and give a simultaneous command and signal to jump as the dog reaches it. The signal arm can be the one holding the object which should be thrown so that it lands just in front of the third hurdle. The dog should be called back, but not over the hurdle, and the exercise should be repeated once more.

3.   Send over hurdles 1 and 2.

The handler and dog are placed a yard back from the up side of the first hurdle. Instruct the handler to send the dog over hurdle number 1 by using a command and signal. As he does so he should throw the object over hurdle number 2 giving a further command to jump as the dog approaches it. If successful the dog should be called back and the exercise repeated twice more. If the dog jumped the first hurdle but ran past the second then you should instruct the handler that more preliminary work must be done before this stage is reached. It may be just a case of repeating stages 1 and 2, or should the dog be running under the second hurdle bar then more work should be done on this part of hurdle training.

4. Send over hurdle 3.

Now place the handler in front of the down side of the second hurdle so that he has his back to it. Instruct the handler to run with his dog towards the third hurdle and give a simultaneous command and signal to jump as the dog reaches it. At the same time the object should be thrown over the hurdle so that it lands at least five yards away. The dog should be called back and the exercise be repeated once more.

5. Send over hurdles 2 and 3.

Now place the handler in front of the first hurdle so that he has his back to it. Instruct him to run with his dog towards the second hurdle and give a simultaneous command and signal to jump as the dog reaches it. As he does so the object should be thrown over hurdle 3 and when the dog has jumped it. The dog should be called back and the exercise repeated once more.

6. Send over hurdles 1, 2, and 3.

If all has gone well so far the time has come to combine all three hurdles. The handler and dog are placed a few yards back from the up side of the first hurdle. Instruct him to send the dog over hurdle number 1 using a command and signal. The dog should be given a further command for hurdle number 2 and, as he rises over it, the object should be thrown over hurdle number 3. A third command to jump should be given as the dog approaches it.

If successful the dog should be called back and the exercise repeated several times more. If the dog jumped the first hurdle but ran past any subsequent ones then you should instruct the handler that more preliminary work must be done before this stage is reached. It may be just a case of repeating previous stages or, should the dog be running under hurdle bars, more work must be done on this part of hurdle training.

Important:

a) If the dog is paying so much attention to his handler that he cannot see the throw by either the handler or instructor then there are two alternatives. Start by lowering the bar of the first hurdle sufficiently to ensure that the dog will not try to run underneath. Next ask the handler to walk round the hurdle and place the ball just in front of the second hurdle, or in front of where it will subsequently be positioned. With a dog that likes to play his eyes should now be upon the ball, and to get it he will have to negotiate a low jump.

If the dog is still intent on looking at his handler then some basic work with teaching the dog to play is necessary before this kind of training work is attempted.

b) If the handler has difficulty throwing the object accurately, and therefore there is a chance that it might roll under the jump in front, it may be necessary to remove that jump(s) in stages 1, 2 or 3. Alternatively it is advisable for the instructor to stand in front of the next hurdle so that he can stop this happening with his foot or body. It could also be that the handler may be mistiming his throw or in general be a very poor thrower. When this is apparent another method is for the instructor to position himself in a suitable position to throw the object himself. The actual position for the instructor to throw from should be determined by the instructor in the light of the handler's and dog's disposition. However it will often be found that an ideal place is just in front and to the side of the of the last hurdle to be jumped.

c) Once the dog has reached the object the handler should have moved out to one side so that he is able to call the dog back without the danger of him jumping back over the hurdles to his handler.

d) Ideally during all stages the handler should not have been allowed to commence these exercises with the dog always on one side. Although the dog is being taught to work on the exercise should randomly commence with the dog on the handlers right and left.

Summary:-

1. Send over hurdle 1.
2. Send over hurdle 2.
3. Send over hurdles 1, and 2.
4. Send over hurdle 3.
5. Send over hurdles 2, and 3.
6. Send over hurdles 1, 2 and 3

★   ★   ★

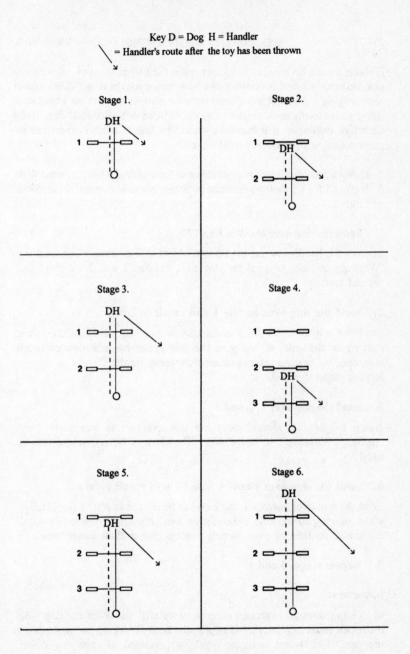

Figure 4. Working on

WORKING ON WITH CONTROL

Handlers must be aware that to just teach their dogs to work on without ensuring that control is retained can be a recipe for disaster. Continually encouraging a dog that has a keen retrieve instinct to work on ahead and using chase motivation to do so can result in an out of control dog. It is therefore important that handlers should be taught control exercises in conjunction with those for working on.

Using a straight line of two hurdles and then adding a third, spaced with 6 - 8 yds. (5.5 - 7.5 metres) distance between, commence control exercises as follows:-

1.   Send the dog over hurdles 1 and 2.

Instruct the handler to use the thrown object as was done when teaching 'Working on' and to send the dog over hurdles 1 and 2. Repeat this several times.

2.   Send the dog over hurdle 1 and recall before 2.

Send the dog over hurdle 1 and as he is jumping, the handler, while moving to the side, should give the dog either his attention or recall command so that he returns rather than jump hurdle 2.
Repeat stages 1 and 2.

3.   Send the dog over 1, 2, and 3.

Again the handler should carry out this exercise as was done when teaching 'Working On' to the dog. The retrieve object should still be used.

4.   Send the dog over hurdles 1 and 2 and recall before 3.

Send the dog over hurdles 1 and 2 and as he descends after 2 the handler, while moving to the side, should give him either his attention or recall command so that he immediately returns rather than jump hurdle 3.

5.   Repeat stages 3 and 4.

Important:

a) Going through exercises once or twice will not teach the dog. An instructor must impress on his pupils that both 'Working on' and adding the control exercises must be regularly practised to have any effect. Teaching the dog to work on without control is a disaster.

b) When we make reference to calling the dog back at no time should he be allowed to return by jumping back over the hurdles. Doing so without having been given such instructions is to allow the dog to learn to jump at random. For some dogs this could be the start of regularly taking their own course. This exercise can be even more likely to teach back jumping than 'Working On' unless the handler moves smartly to one side when recalling their dog.

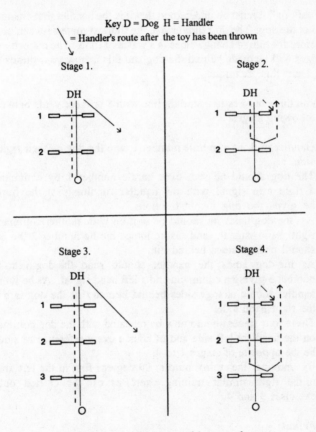

Figure 5. Working on with control

Summary:-

1. Send the dog over hurdles 1, and 2.
2. Send the dog over hurdle 1, and recall before 2.
3. Send the dog over hurdles 1, 2, and 3.
4. Send the dog over hurdles 1, and 2, and recall before 3.

CHANGING SIDES

Teaching handlers right and left side handling on individual obstacles was dealt with in Chapter 2. This chapter looks at the basis of free style handling using three hurdles. It is at this point that your handlers should learn how to change sides so that eventually it will be something that they will do naturally without worrying either them or their dog.

First of all it must be understood that it is the handler that changes side and not the dog. The dog should take the shortest route between obstacles therefore for him to change sides is a waste of time. The majority of side changes will be made behind the dog and this is how your pupils should first learn this technique.

With three hurdles in a straight line with 8 or more yards between use the following stages:

1. Handler in front of hurdle number 1 with the dog on their right hand side.
2. The dog should be sent over hurdle number 1 by command and a right arm signal with the handler running past the hurdle as he gives the dog his instructions.
3. As the dog lands he should be sent on with another command and right hand signal, and as he jumps hurdle number 2 the handler should change sides behind him.
4. As the dog lands the handler should send the dog on to hurdle number 3 giving a command and a left hand signal. As he jumps the handler should change sides behind him so that the dog is back on his right hand side.
5. These four stages should now be repeated with the dog commencing on the handlers left side and of course every reference to sides will be the opposite of stages 1 to 4.
6. By moving the third hurdle 90 degrees first to the left and then to the right similar training exercises can be carried out. See exercises 3 and 4.

Important:

It is critical that instructors should stress to their pupils the importance of body language when these manoeuvres are being undertaken. The handler must not move to change sides until the dog is committed to the obstacle in front. If they do it is likely that the dog will detect his handler's movement and attempt to follow rather than jump. The result of such a mistake is obvious.

Key D = Dog H = Handler

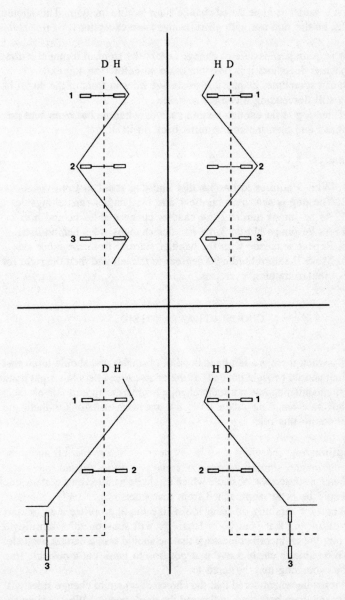

Figure 6. Changing sides - basic exercises

Exceptions:

In first lessons we have stated change sides behind the dog. This should usually be the rule but with all rules there are exceptions.

1. It is quite permissible to change across the front of a tunnel if the handler feels that it is possible to do so before the dog exits.
2. It can sometimes be possible to change sides in front of the dog if he is still descending a contact obstacle.
3. If the dog is far enough behind such as when he has been sent on ahead and then the course turns back on itself.

Summary:-

1. With 3 hurdles in line handler and dog stand in front.
2. The dog is sent over hurdle 1 and the handler runs alongside.
3. As he jumps hurdle 2 the handler changes sides behind him.
4. As he jumps hurdle 3 the handler changes sides behind him.
5. Repeat sequence with the handler starting from the other side.
6. Move the third hurdle 90 degrees to the left and then the right for similar training exercises.

CHOOSING HANDLING SIDES

Usually when there is a left hand bend of obstacles you should teach that handling should be right handed. If the course then alters to a right hand bend the handler should normally change behind the appropriate obstacle into left side handling mode. We use the term usually for there are exceptions to this rule.

Exceptions:-

1. When a subsequent obstacle which might be handled on a certain side would be better approached from that side.
2. When by handling on what looks like the appropriate side to start with means that your body language will subsequently transmit to your dog an incorrect message that he should take a certain obstacle.
3. To be able to easily move into position to mask out a possible trap that your dog may be lured to.
4. It must be remembered that the choice of where to change sides will depend upon both the handler and the dog's speed. What is right for a slower dog may be wrong for one that is faster.

DIRECTIONAL CONTROL FROM BEHIND

Freestyle handling relies very much on signals but there are times when the dog is completely unable to see signals such as when he is working on. On such occasions signals become useless and therefore immediate response to commands are necessary. It is also of great benefit to be able to reinforce signals, designed to turn the dog right and left, with commands even when the dog can see signals. This particularly applies when a dog is working close to the handlers side when the direction in which they must turn might mean crashing into the dogs side.

The most commonly used directional commands are:-

1. 'Back' to turn the dog left.
2. 'This way' to turn the dog right.

Irrespective of the handlers position in relation to their dog the command 'Back' is used each time the dog turns left and 'This way' each time the dog turns right. Obviously different commands can be substituted but they need to be short and not easily confused by the dog with any other commands that he understands. Left and right are too similar with a hard sounding letter T at the end. 'Back' and 'This way' are totally different to each other and the usual agility commands.

To teach handlers how to achieve directional control from behind, first they must understand the importance body language plays with such teaching. If the dog has become used to his handler changing sides then he will usually automatically turn towards where he senses and hears that his handler has moved to.

A dog is far more likely to learn quickly if either 'Back' or 'This way' are taught separately. Once the dog is proficient in one direction then the other direction can be taught. The following exercises should be taught to your pupils:-

1. Set up 3 hurdles in a 3 sided box.
2. The handler and dog should approach the middle hurdle from the closed box side and the dog should be sent on to jump it. As soon as he is committed to jump the handler should move quickly and as far as possible to his left giving the command 'Back'. This should be followed quickly by the chosen jump command.
3. This should be repeated on as many occasions as possible over many training sessions and, as soon as possible, the handler should progressively make less movement until eventually being able to remain still with the dog making his turn upon command.
4. It is probable that the dog will first of all only connect the set-up and turning left habit with immediate surroundings. To counter this

the 3 sided box set-up should be moved around to several different places at the particular training venue and to other venues as well.

5. To reinforce the left turn 'Back' command the handler should be instructed to start using this command in conjunction with a left signal whenever possible.

6. Once the dog thoroughly understands his 'Back' command under varying circumstances and on other equipment then it is time to instruct the handler to teach him to turn right upon command having sent him on to first jump the facing hurdle..

7. Exactly the same procedure and stages are now followed but with the handler moving in the opposite direction and giving the command 'This way'.

8. As soon as possible suggest that the set-up is changed to include other obstacles in different combinations.

9. When the dog has learned 'Back' and 'This way' reliability to these commands, when he is ahead, can be proved by a small three hurdle exercise. place the second hurdle at 90 degree's to the first and the third hurdle at 90 degree's to the second. (See figure 7.)

Important:

Many handlers become confused as to which directional command they should give when their dog is coming towards them. In such cases a right arm signal should be given to turn the dog left in conjunction with the command 'Back'.

When the dog is approaching and he is required to turn right a left arm signal should be given in conjunction with the command 'This way'. In other words it is the direction in which the dog is facing that is important and his association of ideas will be with his command and turning either to his left or right.

Summary:-

1. Set up hurdles in a three sided box.
2. As the dog jumps the middle hurdle the handler moves to the left and gives the command 'Back'.
3. Repeat frequently with less handler movement each time.
4. Move the set-up to different positions and venues.
5. When the dog turns left on a 'Back' command it should always be reinforced with a left signal.
6. Once turning left has been mastered introduce the right turn.
7. Use all procedures above but with the command 'This way'.
8. Use other hurdle combinations
9. Prove reliability with three angled hurdles.

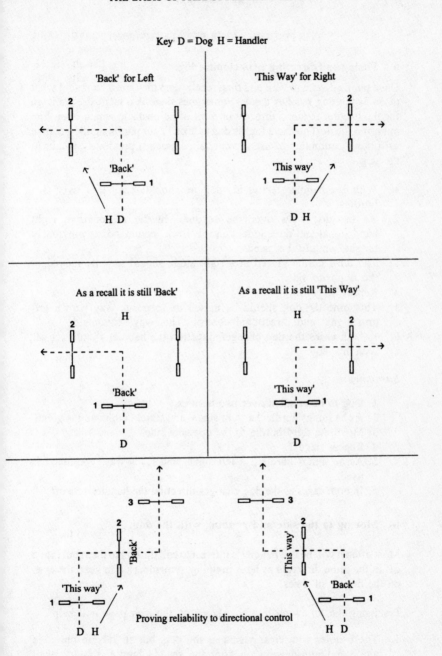

Figure 7. Directional control from behind

CONTINUING AFTER RECALL JUMPING

a)   Facing and directing an oncoming dog.

Once pupils dogs will wait and then recall jump they must be taught what
to do as the dog reaches them. Sometimes there is a tactical advantage
for the handler to stand directly in front of an obstacle which is on line
but is not the next obstacle for the dog to take. Your pupils should practise
as follows continuing to use directional commands previously taught to
the dog:-

1.   With the handler facing his dog he should recall him over two
     hurdles.
2.   As the dog rises over the second hurdle a positive right
     hand signal and directional control 'Back' command, as previously
     taught, should be used.
3.   The third hurdle placed at a right angle should now be moved to
     the opposite side.
4.   Repeat stage 1.
5.   This time the dog should be turned the opposite way with a left
     arm signal and directional control 'This way' command.
6.   In both cases the dog changes direction the handler should set off
     with his dog.

Summary:-

1. Dog to be recalled over two hurdles.
2. As he jumps hurdle 2 a right signal and 'Back' command is given.
3. Move the third hurdle to the opposite side.
4. Repeat stage 1.
5. As he jumps hurdle 2 a left signal and 'This way' command is
   used.
6. In both cases as the dog changes direction the handler sets off.

b)   Moving to the side and running with the dog.

Most often it will be in a handler's interest to call the dog to them but move
off in the same direction as he is jumping, remembering to keep the eyes
on the dog at all times.

Practising the following routines shown on the next page will help:-

1.   The handler with clear vision of the dog, but slightly to one side
     and standing sideways on after the second hurdle, should recall
     the dog over hurdle number 1 towards him.

Using a recall for tactical positioning

Key D = Dog   H = Handler

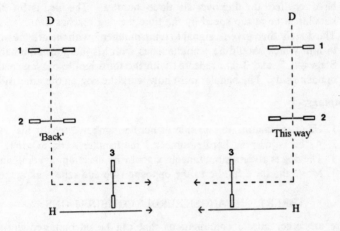

Moving to the side and running with the dog

Key D = Dog   H = Handler

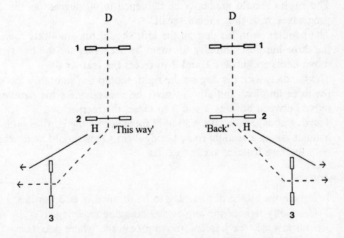

Figure 8. Continuing after recall jumping

2. The dog should be given his jumping command for hurdle number 2 and as he is committed to it the handler should start moving, as fast as possible, towards hurdle number 3. This can be several yards from hurdle number 2 and at sufficient an angle to have made it risky to have recalled the dog over all three hurdles. The idea is for the handler to be at top speed by the time the dog reaches him.
3. The dog is then given a signal to jump number 3 with the arm nearest to him which should be simultaneous with his jumping command.
4. Stages 1, 2, and 3. are repeated with the third hurdle moved to the opposite side. The handler must now work the dog on the other side.

Summary:-

1. Handler standing to one side of hurdle number 2 recalls his dog.
2. As he is jumping hurdle number 2 the handler starts moving.
3. The dog is given a simultaneous signal with his jumping command.
4. Move the third hurdle to the opposite side and repeat all stages.

THREE RIGHT ANGLE HURDLE COMBINATIONS

There are other hurdle combinations that can be encountered during competition which handlers should train for. The first is only a variation of three hurdles in a straight line except that they have been turned at 90 degrees to each other. Practise should be as follows:-

1. Initially the angles should be lessened and the dog recalled over the three hurdles.
2. The angles should gradually be tightened to 90 degrees as the dog progresses with this angled recall.
3. The handler, with his dog on the left, should run smoothly towards the three hurdles. Initially it may be necessary for the handler to move between hurdles 1 and 2 to direct the learner dog.
4. The handler, with his dog on the right, should run smoothly towards the three hurdles. Initially it may be necessary for the handler to move between hurdles 2 and 3 to direct the learner dog.
5. The dog should now take a straight route across the hurdles with the handler taking a straight route beside them. This should be practised with the dog handled on both sides.

Summary:-

1. Lessen the angles for the dog to be recalled over 3 hurdles.
2. Gradually tighten the angles and continue recalling.
3. Run towards the hurdles, moving between where necessary.
4. As 3 above but handling should be on the opposite side.
5. Both dog and handler should now take a straight route.

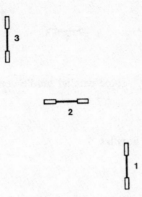

Figure 9. Three right angle hurdle combinations.

THREE PARALLEL HURDLE COMBINATIONS

In the United Kingdom this combination of hurdles is occasionally used in competitions. Unless practised this combination can take the unwary handler by surprise.

1. If necessary place the hurdles at a slightly more helpful angle.
2. The numbers in figure 8 indicate that right side handling should be employed for the first two hurdles.   However, as it is possible to handle both right and left for hurdle number 3, both methods should be practised.
3. By starting on the opposite side of hurdle number 1, left side handling would be most appropriate for the first two hurdles. Once again it is possible to handle on both left and right sides for hurdle number 3, so both methods should be practised.
4. In both 2 and 3 above a side change should also be practised when the dog is committed to the last hurdle. This allows for correct body language should the continuation of a course indicate such tactics.

Summary:-

1. Make the hurdle angles more helpful.
2. The dog should be handled on the right for hurdles 1 and 2.
3. The dog should be handled on the left for hurdles 1 and 2.
4. A side change should also be practised behind the last hurdle.

Figure 10.   Three parallel hurdle combinations.

Working with three hurdles

Summary:-

1. Is the handler using recall jumping where applicable?
2. Is the handler sending the dog ahead to work on?
3. Is the handler able to control the dog when working on?
4. Is the handler changing sides when possible?
5. Is the handler choosing the best side to be on?
6. Is the handler timing his run before the dog reaches him?
7. Is the handler able to directionally control the dog from behind?
8. Is the handler practising three right angle hurdle combinations?
9. Is the handler practising three parallel hurdle combinations?

6

Final Handling Preparation and Sequences

Before allowing handlers to go further with their dogs it is at this point that a good instructor will ensure that they are ready to tackle more involved sequences. It is easy to assume that will be the case but our experience is that bad habits may well start at this point unless you ensure that their handling technique is sound.

COMMANDS AND HAND SIGNALS

While this subject was covered before handlers even commenced individual obstacle training, at that stage invariably the real importance of how commands and signals should be given will not have been apparent. If you have been continually watching your handlers for mistakes in this area so well and good but you must ensure the following:-

1. Commands should be consistent

Once a command has been established that word should be used consistently rather than confuse the dog with several commands which mean the same thing.

2. Commands given concisely

Each command should have a consistent tone although the urgency and volume may vary. All commands should be delivered in a manner that leaves no uncertainty in the dog's mind about what he should do next. It is entirely unnecessary that they should be prefixed with the dog's name indeed, with a quick dog, there is often insufficient time to deliver his name and a command.

3.   Commands are given at the right time.

Handlers may give their commands too soon or too late and the right time can vary from dog to dog and from obstacle to obstacle. For instance some dogs actually jump on command and therefore if the handler does not time the command correctly invariably the dog's leap will be mistimed. When the course turns after a hurdle many dogs can be given the command as they are committed to that hurdle or as they are passing over it. Some however will flatten their trajectory slightly when they hear the command, knocking a hurdle pole down as a result. You must look for this problem and advise when commands are best given.

4.   Commands are given simultaneously with signals.

To be really effective a command and signal combined ensures that the dog knows what is required, but they must be simultaneous.

5.   Commands need not be shouted.

Try and stop unnecessary shouting at an early stage. Most dogs have better hearing than us and do not need to be shouted at. Shouting is usually a product of ineffective early training or handlers trying to improve their dog too quickly. Exasperation of the dog making mistakes leads to shouting as an erroneous attempt to force the message home.

6.   Signals must be positive, not just a flap of the hand.

An arm consistently crisply fully extended and withdrawn will convey to the dog his handler's requirements. Weak floppy hand waves may be acted upon by the dog but it is far better to give a crisp and concise signal that leaves no doubt in the dog's mind about the handler's requirements.

7.   Signals are best given with the hand nearest to the dog.

There are exceptions to this rule on certain tricky parts of a course but basically a fully extended wrong arm across the body is as insignificant as a flapped hand.

8.   Signals should not be too jerky, too quick or left up too long.

All signals must be given smoothly and not so quickly that a blink of the eye can miss them. There is also a chance of incorrect information being transmitted to the dog if they are left up too long. Arms should definitely not be permanently extended. This is often the case and is purely a bad habit the handler has adopted. For the dog it is an equivalent of incessant chatter. For instance a dog working round an inside curve that includes a cross over point with an obstacle that should not be taken will have every right to take that obstacle if the handlers arm is permanently extended as he jumps round the curve. (See figure11 opposite)

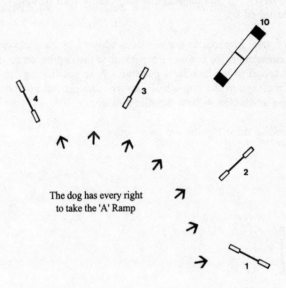

The dog has every right
to take the 'A' Ramp

Figure 11. The danger of a permanently extended arm.

Summary:-

1. Commands should be consistent.
2. Commands must be given concisely.
3. Commands must be at the right time.
4. Commands must be simultaneous with signals.
5. Commands need not be shouted.
6. Signals must be positive not just a flap of the hand.
7. Signals are best given with the hand nearest the dog.
8. Signals should not be too jerky, too quick or left up too long.

BODY LANGUAGE

This becomes increasingly important for handlers who will soon be running courses. If this language is still untidy with waving arms then it must be tidied up.

Also of great importance are positions adopted by handlers under any given circumstance, for the more experienced the dog becomes the more he will respond to his handler's position. Poor positioning can convey a wrong message to the dog while cleverly thought out positioning can be of great assistance to both handler and dog.

The following three figures are some instances:-

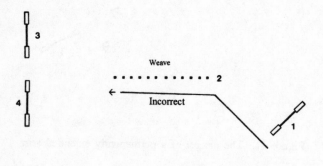

Figure 12. Body language (a)

Handling the above sequence on the right a dog quick out of the weave will pick out jump number 4 rather than jump number 3. This problem is accentuated if there are an even number of weaving poles, which is usually the case in the U.K., for the dog will exit the poles towards jump number 4. At first sight it appears to be the best route but body language is likely to convey an incorrect message by pulling the dog across to the wrong obstacle. A better message would be given with left hand handling at the weaving poles so that as the dog exits his handler can move towards number three as he gives the relevant command.

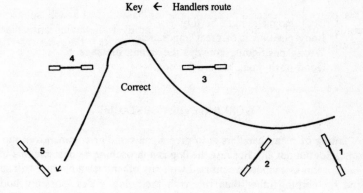

Figure 13. Body language (b)

Almost similar but not quite. Having changed sides as the dog takes hurdle number 3, not only will body language tell the dog to land and turn left it is also an economical handling route.

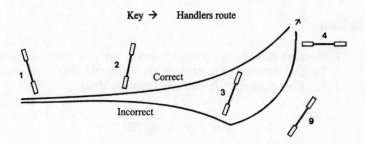

Figure 14. Body language (c)

In the above case handling with the dog on the left at hurdle number 3 will convey all the wrong messages. There would quite likely be a bad collision as the dog lands over hurdle number 3 and the handler tries to turn left. If not the dog would have to have been stopped to allow the handler to move round the hurdle. The tidy and correct way to handle at this point would have been for the handler to have changed sides behind his dog as he was taking number 3 so that his body and voice were correctly positioned to turn the dog straight into hurdle number 4.

Summary:-

1. Body language must be tidy.
2. Body position is of great importance.
3. Wrong positioning conveys the wrong message.
4. Good positioning assists the dog.

WORKING EVERY OBSTACLE

A failing of many handlers is to give signals and/or commands at most obstacles but not all. Because the dog is approaching an obstacle that the handler thinks cannot be confused with any other such a handler will say and do nothing other than run with their dog. Yes, possibly body language will convey something to that dog. However, it is unfair to him when you consider that on many occasions both handler and dog will be approaching a trap and the handler will call the dog away from that obstacle. It is therefore valid for a dog to miss out any obstacle he is not given definite instructions to jump.

An instructor must ensure that at every obstacle definite instructions are given to the dogs.

Summary:-

1. Handlers should give commands and/or signals at every obstacle.
2. To give intermittent commands and/or signals risks confusion.
3. Handlers must not rely on body language alone.

GOING FOR SPEED

Apart from accuracy the other great factor that separates winners from losers is speed. A comfortably paced clear round may suit many people, but there are others who will want to win individual events. Team competitions are not usually all about speed, for it is not always possible to rely on four clear rounds from any given team. Out and out speed is often a recipe for dicing with inaccuracy, and team events are all about accuracy within the judge's time. It is therefore important for an instructor to be able to distinguish early on those handlers who should be concentrating on greater speed from their dogs.

As dogs learn by consistency of habit, with rare exceptions, a dog will learn to work at the speed of his handler. Therefore slow handler slow dog.

It may subsequently be possible to break the habit and increase speed as a replacement habit, but the fact remains that those who want to finish up with a fast dog should be thinking about speed early on in the dog's training. This means that attention should be paid to this facet of training when sequences are first attempted.

Of course slower handlers, by reason of age or fitness, can do much to encourage the dog to be fast by teaching him to work on using motivation such as toys. A lot of ball work over straight lines of hurdles will encourage the retrieve happy dog to work on as long as working on with control is not overlooked. He should also learn how to cut as many corners as possible and move up the course without his dog at the start and at the table, thus conserving energy while still encouraging speed. However the further away from the dog a handler is the harder it is to control him. Those handlers capable of running at speed should use their speed from the beginning of sequencing, but not at the expense of accuracy.

Accuracy comes in many guises. It may be control, and with greater speed control factors may slip. With some dogs more speed can also mean hurdles being knocked down. Contacts missed is a classic problem with speed, for what could be more opposite than speed and keeping the dog on contact areas.

All these problems can be avoided if initial training has been carried out thoroughly before proceeding to sequences or complete rounds. It is when a handler has been allowed to progress too fast, specifically on the above training facets, that problems occur when adding in the speed factor.

There is also the danger of the naturally fast dog being made to wait for his slow handler when straight line sequences are first attempted. Most dogs have a secure distance from their owners when taken for a walk. This is why training clubs will teach handlers to retreat from the dog, rather than to chase him, when calling one who is not responding to his recall command. Translated into Agility, when the dog gets ahead of his secure distance he looks back for his handler. In the first place this is a habit to avoid, and in the second it is likely to teach the dog to circle for that is how he will complete his turning back movement.

One way to avoid this problem is to ask a faster experienced handler to work the dog at this stage, for the danger is that if the handler is consistently a long way behind his dog that dog will soon slow to his handler's speed and that will become his habit.   It should not be necessary for the faster handler to work the dog forever more but rather is should be seen as a short transitional period where the dog learns to keep going fast.

Sequences with curves in them will allow the slower handler to cut corners and still retain the dog's speed, but for long straight or slightly curved lines it is essential that the dog does not learn the wrong habit.

There is no doubt that because Agility, to a certain extent, relies upon an ability to run there is an athletic factor. Where a handler is capable of exploiting that athletic factor then he should be encouraged to do so.

There is also a danger of a faster handler trying to work the dog at heel, but that is counter productive and should always be discouraged by an instructor. Those who can sprint should do so but still be encouraged to leave their dogs at the start, change handling sides at will and cut corners. In such a way they will be employing all the tactics of a slower handler yet doing so at a greater speed. If this has been combined with sound initial training so that speed is not an incentive for the dog to make mistakes then we have a potential winner.

Of course there are those mistaken judges who think they can slow Agility down by building tricky courses and in this way the speed factor is nullified. Experience has proved this to be a fallacy, for the handler and dogs usually win but do so in a stuttering, boring style. What is so often overlooked is that dogs handled very fast have extremely quick reactions to commands and therefore over a tricky course they still come out the winners. It just proves there is no substitute for quick responses from the dog and that is only possible when good control has been apparent before Agility training commenced.

SEQUENCES

Having learned each individual obstacle a dog should not be asked to attempt full courses without some intermediary practise. This we believe is best done by setting up short sequences for learner handlers and dogs to practise on. This part of training should probably be continued for several weeks before handler and dog are ready to attempt a full course.

The following pages list many combinations of sequences that will serve various training purposes but instructors should use their own imagination to build sequences that suit any dogs particular stage of training. It must also be remembered that a competition dog can often be helped with a problem by reverting to sequences that are applicable to the problem or it's solution.

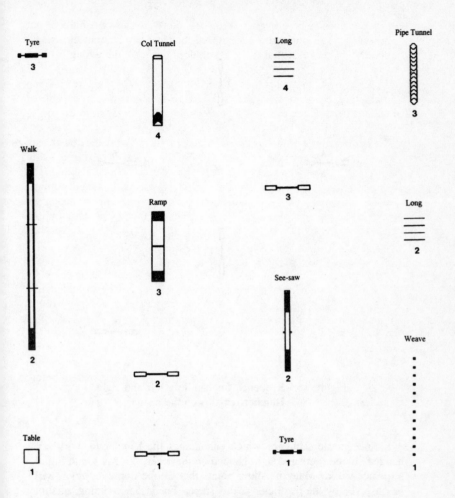

Figure 15.   Four straight line sequences.

This illustration shows four very basic straight line sequences and all can be worked both ways providing that the see-saw, long jump and collapsible tunnel are turned round. These sequences include all the usual obstacles to be found on an Agility course and are ideal for basic sequence work that includes all obstacles but does not require the dog to negotiate more than four in any sequence. They can of course be varied to suit the dogs under training or obstacles available. The whole point is that they are basic sequences being in a straight line and only contain three or four obstacles.

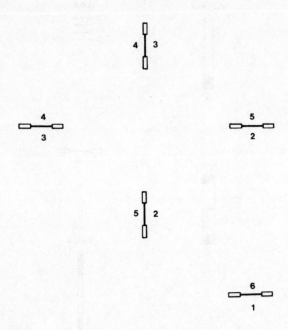

Figure 16.   Sequence for handling left and right.
Handler remains on the inside.

A simple hurdle sequence which encourages the handler to work left handed on one route and right handed on the other. This is sound initial sequence work. Many handling points that can be improved upon will be observed by the instructor at this stage. For instance timing, quality and consistency of commands and signals are immediately apparent as is body position. For a new handler it is inevitable that many of these points will need to be discussed at this stage.

Note that no side changes are required it is simply a sequence to be used to get a handler and dog moving from one obstacle to the next and in this context it is very basic. Incorporated in it is the opportunity for the dog to be left at the start and recalled to the handler but this technique would only be used if it has already been taught. Even if used the instructor will also want to see the handler's and dog's ability to start together at the beginning. There may also be handling faults at the start to be pointed out.

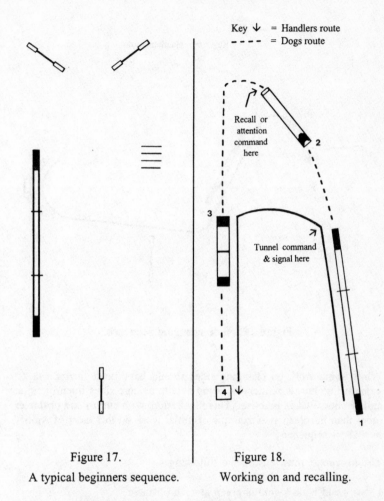

Key ↓ = Handlers route
- - - - = Dogs route

Recall or
attention
command
here

2

3

Tunnel command
& signal here

4 ↓

1

Figure 17.	Figure 18.
A typical beginners sequence.	Working on and recalling.

Figure 17 shows a short course which gives the beginner handler the chance to practise course curves while including some obstacles other than hurdles. Again it would be possible to use this sequence either way.

Figure 18 is designed specifically to encourage a handler to use working on and recalling techniques other than at the start or pause, this sequence illustrates these techniques obvious use. Instructors must ensure that handlers do not move towards the 'A' ramp too soon Exactly when will depend upon the dog and stage of training but there is a danger of him following the handlers body movement if he does moves too soon.

Key ←   Handlers route

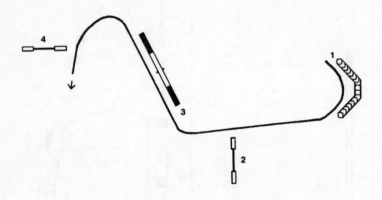

Figure 19. Side changing sequence.

While some work on changing sides should have been carried out on straight line hurdle sequences, being able to change sides fluently on an agility course takes practise. This illustration, with curves and obstacles other than hurdles, is an example of initial work on this facet of Agility in a short sequence.

The instructor must ensure the following:-

1. A good hand signal is given at each obstacle.
2. That the dog is definitely committed to the see-saw with at least both paws upon it before he attempts his side change or the dog will be distracted and likely to move towards him.
3. The handler should now move smoothly along the side of the see-saw parallel with his dog while he is told to pause for the tip and is subsequently given his contact instruction.
4. Determined by the exact position of the see-saw in relation to the hurdle that follows it may be necessary for the handler to move his dog on forward a little so that there is a reasonable curve to hurdle number 4 as opposed to a sharp angle which may not be helpful.

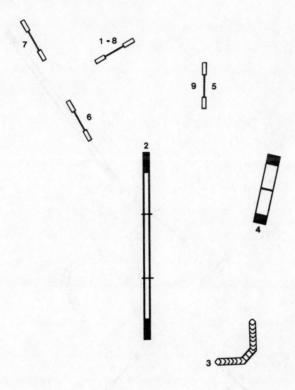

Figure 20. Cross over sequence with change of sides.

One of the most common handling problems to be encountered on an Agility course is the cross over sequence. This is a point where there are often choices of obstacles for the dog to take. Figure 20 shows a seven obstacle sequence that allows the handler to practise this problem. Body position is often of vital importance in a cross over situation.

Obstacles 1 to 2 could either be worked as a recall or by left or right handed handling. However the start is worked, the dog will need to be on the handlers right for the dog walk. The handler must be warned that from 5 to 6 the dog may pick out obstacle number 1 therefore body language and commands are going to be crucial. The following change of sides once the dog is committed to 6 is also very important.

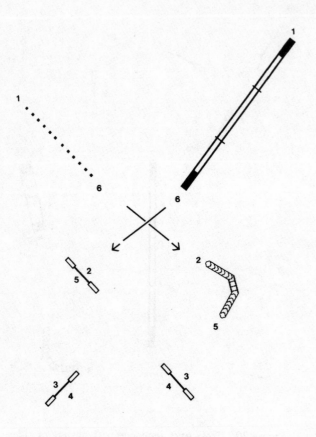

Figure 21. Cross over sequence.

Another example of a cross over sequence but this one can be worked
three ways. It should be worked two or three times using the tunnel as
obstacle number 2. This will have imprinted in the dog's mind the route
he is to take. However now will be a good testing time to gauge whether
his response to commands is greater than his desire to take the route he
has previously taken. This can be done by using the hurdle as obstacle
number 2. When the third change of route takes place the handler will
need to be quick with his command at the end of the dog walk for a hurdle
is now the second obstacle. This sequence can be useful in a class
situation where several dogs can try each route several times.

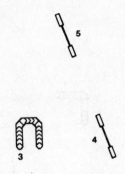

Figure 22. Sequence for changing sides across the front of a tunnel.

On the majority of occasions changes of sides are carried out behind the dog and very often as he is committed to jump. There are several exceptions to this rule and figure 22 shows an opportunity to cross in front of the tunnel while the dog is inside it. It is preferable if the dog has just come round the tunnel bend when the handler passes across the front of it. In such a way he will know where to move to as he exits. Combined with the handlers command and a positive right hand signal to hurdle number four the dog will have been picked up on the right and directed to jump the next hurdle.

It will be necessary for the handler to pass a little way past number four and then direct the dog by hand signal, voice and body movement as they both curve towards hurdle number 5 from the opposite direction to that in which they took the previous one.

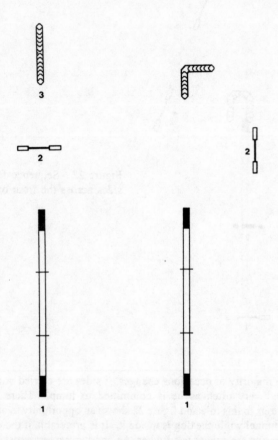

Figure 23. Tunnel problem sequences

An inexperienced dog can be caught out after descending a dog walk or
see-saw so that his eyes are looking under a single pole hurdle at an inviting
tunnel. An experienced fast dog needs to be practised on sequences similar
to that shown on the right of the above illustration using the tunnel as a
trap. Unless the handler has perfect control the dog may choose to take
the tunnel.

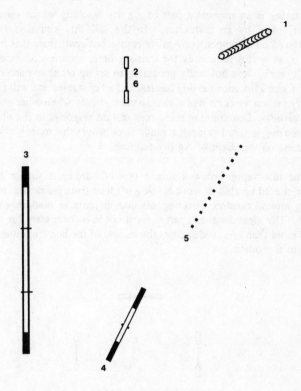

Figure 24. Sequence with a trap at the end.

An example of a possible course situation where the tunnel is a trap for
the unwarry handler. This illustration shows how the dog can be drawn
towards the tunnel unless the handler is quick to give a good responding
dog his instructions. If the dog is working on the handler's left at the
weaving poles then they may have a chance of moving across the front
of their dog as he exits thus blocking the route to the tunnel. This however
is not the way we advise. If the dog has been taught to weave on the
handlers right hand side and the handler has no need to be running tight
to the poles, then as the dog exits, the handler can make a more
pronounced move towards hurdle number 6 while he gives a firm 'Back'
or attention command. Like figure 23. figure 24. should also be practised

BOX TRAINING

Box training is an important part of Agility teaching which should not be overlooked by an instructor. In the UK this situation is often encountered on a competitive Agility course but apart from that it is one of the most useful sequences for training basic control combined with obstacle work. It is not really necessary to set up other obstacles in the shape of a box for once the dog has learned all obstacles and will respond instantly on box work he will also respond instantly when other obstacles are involved. Box training reinforces instant response to the obstacles which the dog is asked to jump at random, or proves that more work needs to be done on this facet of Agility training.

In the illustration below a simple box of hurdles is shown and the handler should be able to work his dog off lead from inside and also, by moving around outside, directing his dog to jump at randomly chosen hurdles. The ideal distance apart is for it not to be necessary for the dog to take more than one stride across the middle of the box from one facing hurdle to the other.

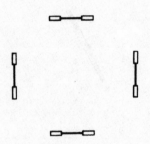

Figure 25. Box training.

Should the dog be slow to turn back after jumping from the inside to the outside then some lightweight line work may be advantageous to illicit a faster response from the dog. To use this technique, as the dog lands from a hurdle, gentle pressure should be applied to the line so that the dog must immediately turn. While this is done the dog's attention command should simultaneously be given and as he responds he should be praised. In this way the dog will learn to turn back immediately the command is given. This type of training is not recommended for beginners as it requires skilled line handling within the box if the lead is not to be caught around a hurdle or the dog's legs .

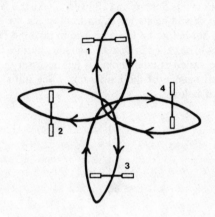

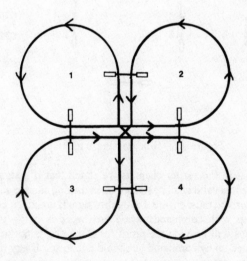

Figure 26. Some suggested box training patterns

When handler and dog are really proficient at work in and around a box of hurdles and the dog's response is instantaneous, then some additional inviting obstacles can be strategically placed on the outside of the box. The two tunnels and a tyre are ideal for this training, and to prove real reliability the dog should be worked as follows. He should be sent over a hurdle from inside the box and allowed to take the facing obstacle. Following this he should be started again from inside the box, sent over the same hurdle, but before he has a chance to take the facing obstacle again the dog should be called back to take another hurdle. These training sequences can be varied at random and if felt necessary other obstacles can be substituted outside of the hurdle box. See initial set up in the illustration shown below.

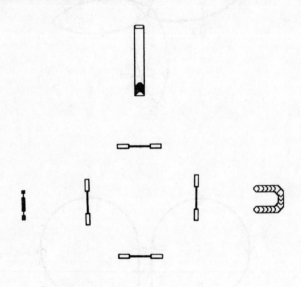

Figure 27.   Box training with traps.

Remember that in the earlier chapters we stated that if a signal is valid at one obstacle it is valid at all obstacles when the dog can see such signals. As an instructor you must ensure that quality signals are given consistently and backed up with commands while box work is being undertaken. These exercises will provide the proof for if the dog is not told to jump by signal backed up by command he should not do so. Every time a jump is taken without instruction training has taken a backward step. Therefore to allow a handler to practise box work and not to insist on signals at every obstacle is to invite uncertainty in the dog's mind.

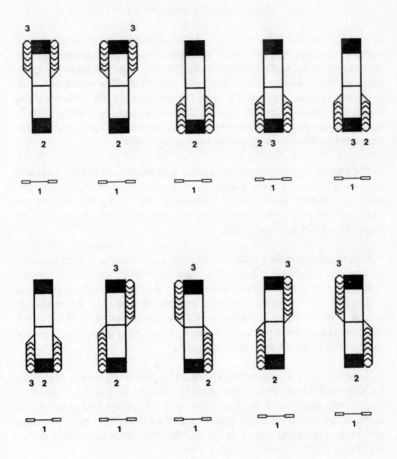

Figure 28. 'A' ramp and tunnel problems.

There are many combinations of 'A' ramp and tunnel that a judge can use. Figure 28 shows the most common basic combinations to be found. All should be practised so that the dog and handler new to competition are not caught unaware when faced with such possibleproblems.

While we would not necessarily recommend that some of these combinations are used by judges, for the reason that they can turn a competition into a lottery, they are to be encountered and therefore practise is necessary.

FULL COURSE SEQUENCES

Once handlers and dogs are deemed by the instructor to be ready to tackle complete courses then it follows that simple ones should at first be used. At this stage there will probably still be handling improvement to be made although the course demands very little. What would be wrong is for the instructor to build a trappy course which immediately has the learner dog taking the wrong jumps. Remember that a dog learns by habit and every wrong course is a lesson that the dog has had in getting it wrong. Far better that difficulty is gradually increased slowly.

Of course when it comes to regular competition handlers, complete courses will have a large part to play in their practise work and your critique. While these type of sequences and complete courses are suggested for beginners there is no reason why experienced handlers and dogs should not also use them.

One of the problems with agility training classes is time wasted building or rebuilding courses. Figure 29, shown opposite, shows a suggested training set-up with 20 obstacles that can be used for individual sequences and/or full courses without moving equipment around. When such a course is used for sequencing, two or three groups can be working at the same time on different parts and, if necessary, a further group of new pupils can be instructed on individual obstacles.

This set-up is a suggestion as we have previously stated that each training club has to tailor their training sessions to suit the amount of equipment, numbers of handlers, dogs and instructors available. What is important is that whatever system a club adopts a little prior planning will make maximum use of facilities. So remember our advice at the beginning of the manual and plan your class.

The opposite illustration allows for the following combinations:-

7-13-14-16-20 - Working on and recall jumping.
13-14-17 - Directional work with dog turning right.
13-14-15 - Directional work with dog turning left.
14-15-16-17 - Box work all combinations.
8-9-10-5-6 - Left handling. - 6-5-10-9-8 - Right handling.
10-4 and 5-4 - Sending dog to weave poles from both sides.
6-5-10-11-3-2 - Two side changes when dog is committed to 10 and 3.
2-19-17-14 - One side change when dog is committed to 17.
3-11-12-18 - Using number 17 as a trap.
Full course route (a) 1-18-12-10-5-6-8-9-10-4-11-12-17-14-15-16-20
Full course route (b) 19-17-14-13-7-8-9-10-5-6-7-13-14-17-18-1

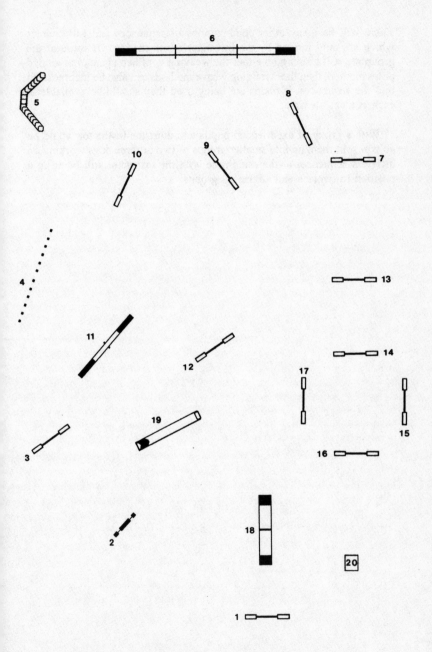

Figure 29. Sequencing and complete course multi routes

There will be many other combinations of sequences and full courses which are only limited by the instructor's imagination. If some of the group are still training on either the weaving confined channel or angled poles method, then these training weave methods can also be incorporated into the sequences. If hoops are being used they should be available at each contact obstacle.

With a group of experienced pupils and dogs the instructor would be able to split them up into smaller groups of two or three dogs working on different sequences at the same time with the instructor still being in a position to oversee and advise all groups.

7

The Competition Class

Many club instructors are quite proficient at teaching handlers and dogs how to master the obstacles. However when it comes to advising handlers on improving their handling and dogs performance, it is our experience that this is where there is often weakness.

One of the problems is that sometimes the instructor is expected to advise a handler who maybe has greater experience than himself, or perhaps wins many more prizes. Yes of course it is easier to instruct if all handlers in a class accept their instructor as the best competition handler in the club or their past experience and results means they are held in high esteem. Whilst we have pointed out in the early part of this manual the attributes of an agility instructor, the reader will remember that it says nothing about being a prolific prize winner. Of the 12 points we list only the first two relate to experience, and they are:-

1. To have a comprehensive knowledge of the sport and it's rules.
2. To have had considerable agility handling experience.

Providing that instructors qualify under the above two points they should not feel unable to advise competition handlers, even if they are already prolific winners. The best sportsmen in the world are still taught and criticised where necessary, and an agility handler who thinks that they know it all and can do no wrong should quit while they are ahead. Watch most major sporting events and you will find that the top stars have coaches or advisors. In many cases these coaches achieved less in competition than the champion they now advise. If this holds good for other sports then it must surely do so for agility.

DIVIDING HANDLERS BY STANDARD AND SAVING TIME

It is not easy to advise on whether there should be one training class for Starters and another for Seniors. It really is a question of how much time, space and equipment a club may have.

With large numbers of competitive handlers in a class there is an argument for two or even three instructors to be giving their critiques on dog and handlers performance. This can save a lot of time and ensure that each handler is given a thorough appraisal of their round. The next round can be taking place with a second instructor watching while the first instructor gives his critique to the first handler.

Clubs must tailor classes to suit the numbers and standards of members. Individual and private instructors will probably work on a more personal basis.

CLASS STRUCTURE.

In our opinion it is best first to set up a competition type course for handlers and that they should not be allowed to practise on any other equipment until they have completed at least one such round. This is the best way to simulate competition conditions so that handling errors become more apparent. If they are allowed to practise first then everything becomes that more familiar to the dog who will start acting from memory rather than relying on handler control.

If handlers use specific contact methods, such as a lure or a 'Down' on or at the end of contact areas, then they should be allowed to do so during any simulated competition rounds. Other than this gesture to training everything else should be treated as competition. Prior to their run handlers should walk the course, as they do in competition, planning how they will handle while remembering the route.

During these runs a good instructor will have to remember many errors or areas where handling improvement can be made. If it is thought that there are likely to be many areas of improvement to be pointed out then it is not a bad idea to ask someone to stand with you so they can quickly write down headlines of the points you will wish to discuss with the handler. Once you have decided upon areas for improvement handlers should be practising a particular obstacle or sequence where you have noted weaknesses.

BUILDING THE RIGHT COURSES

It is important that the instructor should build suitable practise courses for his class. It may be that they need to be simple or possibly they may need to be difficult. Remember that although you may dislike trappy courses there are judges out there who will build in this manner. Your handlers should practise on such courses or they will be ill equipped when faced with them.

RUNNING COURSES WITHOUT
ALLOWING THE DOG TO NEGOTIATE OBSTACLES

As a control exercise there is nothing like asking handlers to run their dog around a course without allowing him to negotiate any obstacles. Body language should tell the dog that the next jump is likely to be required to be taken but at the last minute he is called away. This therefore reinforces the idea in the dog's mind that although an obstacle may be just in front of him he must not take it unless he is given instructions to do so.

Handlers should not give any signals or any indication that an obstacle is to be negotiated as it would only serve to confuse. It is just a test to see if the dog is more responsive to being called away from obstacles after he has fixed them with his eye.

WEAVING IMPROVEMENT

It is almost certain that no handler will have a perfect weave that cannot be improved upon. A handler may argue that their dog never makes a mistake but several areas where improvement can be made should be looked for. It may be a question of speed, working on into the poles, entry from any angle, and many other facets of weaving that could be sharpened up. Maybe the dog may not rely on the handler being alongside but just how far away from the weaving poles can the handler be before his dog becomes confused by his absence?

It is therefore a good idea to have an additional set of practise weaving poles so that handlers can take turns in improving their dogs weaving technique. (See 'A Comprehensive List of Agility Problems' in the next chapter) If necessary even an experienced handler should be advised to start at the beginning again to overcome a specific problem that is obstructing further weaving improvement.

CRITIQUES OF COMPLETE ROUNDS.

There is no doubt about it that what all competition handlers like best of all is running complete rounds. Now there is definitely an argument for them doing so as long as this type of training is not overdone. When complete rounds are practised it should be with a view to handler and dog improvement. Therefore the instructor should watch carefully to see where improvements are possible.

This is the area of instruction where the authors feel most instructors are at their weakest, yet it is here that handlers and dogs can be made into champions by a good coach. Even though other club members may win more prizes in agility than the instructor he should never fear giving them constructive advice. Remember that everyone needs a coach for it is impossible to see all of ones own mistakes.

Maybe up until now you have wondered what instruction you can give to skilled partnerships of dog and handler. If that is so we would suggest that you digest the following information and you will soon find that there are many points to look for. For a concise list move straight to the summary at the end of this section.

1.   Commands

The handler may be giving too many commands. Maybe they are delivered too loud, too early or too late. Maybe they are not obeyed, or there might be a tone of command problem.

2.   Signals

Signals are rarely well used and it is amazing how many handlers do not think to use the arm nearest the dog. Then again they are often of poor quality, sometimes more akin to a wet piece fish being flopped around rather than a definite arm signal. Many handlers get into a bad habit of running round with an arm permanently extended. This takes away the impact of a signal delivered at the right time and can be likened to subjecting the dog to incessant chatter during his round. Once a decision has correctly been made to use signals as a handling method, then they should be given at every obstacle even though the next or subsequent obstacles are obvious to the dog. Remember that sometimes an obvious obstacle is not the next one to be negotiated and we do not signal to such an obstacle. It would therefore be valid for the dog not to take an obstacle that has not been signalled.

3. Changing sides

Good agility handlers change handling sides at will. Remember that it is the handler that changes sides, not the dog. There cannot be any golden rule as to where and if a handler should change sides for it very much depends upon the handler and dog's speed. What might be dangerous for one partnership if a side change is not made at a given point will not necessarily effect another.

The whole point of changing sides is to save a handler unnecessary running and to keep body language and positioning correct for their dog. Having stated that, the most usual place to change sides is behind the dog as he commits to an obstacle. If the handler moves across too soon the dog can become confused and try to follow rather than take the obstacle. Changes can also be too late, leaving the handler tucked too close to an obstacle. Another problem is choosing an inappropriate place to change sides, which then transmits the wrong body language to the dog who moves in relation to his handler and is then wrongly placed for the next obstacle. There may be an obvious place to change sides, and whilst dog and handler are capable of effecting the manoeuvre, for some reason they do not carry it out. Of course there are still a few handlers around that insist on running with the dog on the left the whole way round. This is to be discouraged for it is too time and energy consuming.

4. Body language

Handlers body language means much to an agility dog. For a start if the body is in the wrong position the dog will not have a positive indication of where or what is next. Some handlers run around like windmills with arms and legs flying everywhere. Untidy body language does not help at all, and again conflicting messages may be being given to the dog. Another problem is too quick movements by a handler. While for some dogs just a slight head, leg or arm movement can tell the dog to get off a contact obstacle, other handlers may actually take off too soon causing the dog to jump off. Being too late to move away might mean the dog shooting ahead and taking a wrong course.

5. Weaving

Does the dog work on ahead into the poles? Will he enter from extreme angles? Is he reliant on the handler's presence beside him? In other words unless the handler is in position he will not weave and will stop doing so unless they follow along with him. Will the dog only weave when the handler is on the dog's left, for some courses will lend themselves to the handler weaving when the dog is on the handler's right.

6. Praise

Incorrect use of praise is often a fault. It can be given at the wrong time or in an incorrect tone, then of course some do not give any praise at all.

7. Contacts

First of all for consistent success, particularly with fast dogs, it is necessary to have a method of keeping the dog on contacts. Such a method should have been consistently trained. Maybe the method is not being properly applied or it is not working consistently. Then again perhaps the handler has no real method or is inadvertently signalling the dog to move off too soon. Another problem can be when the handler's 'Wait' or similar command becomes a command to the dog to jump off. If a dog is only making contact with just a few inches or centimetres of a contact in training this will inevitably result in missed competition contacts. There is no time for a dog to be taught to stop on any contact obstacle, and the top of the 'A' ramp is a classic example. Handlers with dogs that are slow over such obstacles will need advice on how to gain more speed. It may just be a question of confidence or maybe play training will help such a dog.

8. Control

There can be many such commands under the general heading of control which generally have nothing to do with agility at all, and neither should they be trained for during agility. Maybe the handler cannot leave his dog at the start for fear that he will move. Alternatively he is left but then anticipates being called up. Often dogs have a poor response to attention or turning commands and this is when they take the wrong course. At the table many problems are obvious, such as a dog who will not go down on one command, goes down too slowly or the handler corrects the down on the table. Very few handlers are able to reposition themselves to advantage during a table count because they dare not leave the dog.

9. Control when ahead

Many handlers are unable to turn their dog left or right when he is ahead of them, or else they think he understands but the dog does not respond to the command.

10. In general

A mistake that everyone makes sooner or later is to take their eyes off the dog. This is generally when he will go wrong. Another is to turn their back onto the dog. Perhaps they are too casual or too formal, or even have the wrong footwear or clothing. If the dog will not work on ahead precious time can be lost. Watch out for food being incorrectly used during training; it is common fault. There are so many problems that can be apparent but few instructors seem to be aware of them or are afraid to point them out to the more prolific winners in their club. Listed below is a summary of many points to look for when instructing competition handlers, but for a concise list of problems refer to chapter 8.

Summary:-

Commands

1. Too many commands.
2. Commands given too early.
3. Commands given too late.
4. Commands that are too loud.
5. Commands not obeyed.
6. Commands with a tone problem.

Signals

1. Signals of poor quality.
2. Continuous signals.
3. Signals not given at every obstacle.
4. Signals given with the wrong arm.

Changing sides

1. Changing too late.
2. Changing too soon.
3. Changing at the wrong place.
4. No change made when appropriate.
5. Handler never changes.

Body language

1. Wrong positioning.
2. Untidy body language.
3. Moving on too soon.
4. Moving on too late.

Weaving

1. Dog is reliant on the handlers presence.
2. Dog will only weave with handler on one side.
3. Dog will not work ahead into the poles.
4. Problems with entrances from an angle.

Praise

1. Praise is used incorrectly.
2. No praise is given.

Contacts

1. No method is employed by the handler.
2. The employed method is not working.
3. The employed method is not properly applied.
4. Handler is teaching anticipation to move off.
5. A command to stay on has become a command to get off.
6. Insufficient contact made during practise.
7. The dog is stopping on contact obstacles.
8. The dog is slow over contact obstacles

Control

1. Handler cannot leave his dog at the start.
2. Handler cannot leave his dog at the table.
3. When left the dog anticipates the start.
4. Dog is being taught to anticipate the start.
5. Handler must hold dog at the start.
6. Dog is slow into the table down.
7. Handler psychically corrects the table 'Down'.
8. The dog has a poor response to a turning command.

Control when ahead

1. No ability to command a right turn.
2. No ability to command a left turn.
3. No response to directional commands.

General

1. The dog will not work on.
2. Handler takes his eyes off the dog.
3. Handler turns his back on the dog.
4. An obstacle has not been properly taught.
5. The handler is too casual.
6. The handler is too formal.
7. There is an incorrect use of food.
8. Handler is poor at tactical positioning.
9. Unsuitable clothing.
10. Unsuitable or unsafe footwear.

8

A Comprehensive List of Agility Problems

In the previous section we listed some of the points that a good instructor will look for when competition handlers are practising. Many are common errors but now we are listing specific problems that a dog or handler might have. We make no apology for the fact that a few are the same as those listed in 'Critiques of complete rounds' the point being that the following is an attempt to cover as many problems as possible.

Before offering advice it is very helpful to know how the problem occurred. Instructors with experience will know that it is unlikely that a handler will recognise how their problem occurred. Once a reason why any given behaviour has been established, finding the best possible remedial action is always much more likely. If it is a common fault then an instructor can quickly make an educated guess as to why.

If all the handlers in the class, or club, have been brought to their present handling capabilities by your expert guidance then we are sure that you will not have any problems to deal with. However, this does not allow for the existing agility handler who joins you from another club particularly because your fame has spread. Then there are occasions when you may have guest handlers at your training sessions.

Let us not forget the agility instructor who might be working on their own and not be part of a club set up. They are no different for to be a good instructor of the sport you must have awareness of problems and of how to better an existing good partnership.

We list below many problems that you may encounter but are sure you will be asked to solve others. They may be variations on our list so that the answer or part of it is contained herewith. If you come across others or find better remedies by all means tell us for one of the aims of this manual is to share knowledge.

FITNESS AND SAFETY

1. Is the dog's movement sound?

If an instructor feels that the movement of one of his pupils dogs is unsound then he should be asking questions about it and giving advice as to whether or not that dog should continue with Agility training. It may be something simple like a thorn in a pad, or that the dog's poor movement is permanent. Of course where necessary veterinary advice should be sought, but above all the instructor should ensure that the dog is not suffering by practising Agility.

2. Is the dog overweight?

Advice should always be given about overweight dogs and not just because their owners want to play Agility with them. A fat dog has his life shortened but it is not fair to ask him to jump and perform feats of Agility if he is seriously overweight. More exercise and less food is often the answer, or maybe the dog is continually receiving too many and too large tit-bits whether it be for training purposes or just for being there.

3. Is the dog too young or too old?

In Chapter 1 we discussed the age at which a dog should commence Agility training and rather than go over that ground again it is better that reference is made to that item.

Certainly there is no point in old dogs being taught Agility, particularly those that have led a sedentary life thus far. Far better that advice is given that any particular dog should be allowed to grow old gracefully while the handler decides about another dog for Agility.

There has to come a time when a dog must be retired from Agility and that should be before he shows signs of stiffness or that he is starting to struggle when practising. It is a difficult decision for handlers to make for often their dog appears to be working well. Watch out for the little tell tale signs and where necessary have a chat with the handler about retiring his dog soon. Most handlers will get it right anyway for it is a poor one who wants to be seen competing with a dog that is struggling because of age.

4. Is the handler fit?

The first thing to remember is that, within reason, everyone of any age is entitled to have a go at Agility so age should not be a deterrent. Unfortunately old age might go hand in hand with infirmity which indicates a lack of fitness. Many handlers over the age of sixty still compete and some are quite fit, with Agility helping them to retain such fitness. This of course is a good thing. There have been and still are others over the age of 70 who are competing, so we must discount old age altogether and only consider fitness.

An unfit handler will easily be seen and the instructor should decide whether their fitness is something he should mention or leave well alone. Suffice it to say that an instructor is in charge of his class and should therefore be awake to any possible personal injury problems because of a lack of fitness.

5. Is the right footwear being worn?

The most important point is to ensure that handlers do not necessarily fall. Agility, particularly when it is at speed, is all about twisting and turning, and handlers that slip and fall can injure themselves or their dog. For this reason we advise that trainer shoes with studs that allow grip on slippery surfaces should be used. There is an argument for two different types of trainers to be kept and chosen for applicable surfaces. One should be for the slippery surfaces and include studs and here we would recommend the cricket shoe trainer or some may prefer a hockey shoe. The other would not have studs and would possible be used when on a carpeted surface.

6. Is the equipment safe?

Just as a judge must be responsible for equipment safety in his ring so should the instructor have a similar responsibility for equipment he expects his handlers dogs to traverse. There should be no chance of poor equipment causing injury to handler or dog. Particular care should be taken to ensure that nothing protrudes that is sharp which could catch the dog, or that stakes used under higher pieces of equipment do not have pointed ends. Obviously such points would be dangerous if a dog fell.

7. Is the course ready for the dog?

It is all too easy to forget that the previous dog twisted the collapsible tunnel or that there are hurdle poles that need to be replaced. Where necessary ensure that tunnels are properly secured and this usually applies before the first dog runs. Use one or two class members as stewards if necessary.

THE DOG

8. Is the dog the right material for Agility?

While nearly all breeds can take part in Agility, particularly the small ones who are adequately catered for as minis, extremely large breeds might have some difficulty. If a large dog is capable and willing to try then there is no reason why he could not take part, however we do have to be realistic and suggest that if the aim is to win prizes then an extremely large breed may be unsuitable.

9. Is the dog nervous of strangers?

One of the finest ways to overcome a dogs fear of strangers is where there are people with dogs. It is our experience that a dog nervous of people relaxes far more quickly when strangers have dogs with them. It is a behavioural problem and the more handlers of such dogs mix in dog training or breed activities the better. It is all part of the socialising that they need to rehabilitate them. However dog owners can be a nervous dog's worse enemy for they will want to force themselves upon him in a belief that he should like them. Such an approach is entirely wrong and the instructor should ensure that every class member knows how nervous dogs should be treated. The ideal is for strangers not to make any eye contact with the dog and definitely not push hands towards him. Far better to allow the dog to make friends in his own time than to allow well intentioned but ill informed people to thrust themselves upon such a dog.

10. Is the dog nervous of other dogs?

Whilst generally speaking it is better to get nervous dogs to face up to their fears in small controlled doses, in this case a dog nervous of other dogs needs to be protected from any that show the slightest signs of aggression. To have a new nervous dog attend for the first week only to be set upon by the class bully is not conducive to helping that dog overcome his fears. Plenty of exposure to the dogs well adjusted with other canines is what is required. Again this should be carried out in a matter of fact manner without the nervous dog being unwillingly forced towards others.

11. Is the dog nervous of thunder and bangs?

The dog that is nervous of sudden noise such as gunshot, thunder or similar will be absolutely fine until he hears the sound, then anything can happen. If he is working at the time he might run off in a panic, and we have known instances where a dog has gone for miles before he has stopped. At best he will lay his ears flat and not be able to work again for some considerable time. This problem can be very difficult to cure and the best way is to have a recorded audio tape of such sound and then commence playing it to the subject at a very low barely audible level while he is played with. Gradually over a period of weeks the sound should be fractionally increased whilst games continue. Eventually it should be possible to play the tape quite loudly without the dog reacting. One thing owners of such dogs should be counselled about is that they should never try and soothe the dog that is in fright. Unfortunately the dog, being unable to understand our intentions, is likely to regard our soothing tones and actions as identical to that which we use when we are praising him for doing the right thing. It is far better that an attitude of "problem, what problem?" is adopted. In this way we, as superior members of the pack, are showing that we are not frightened and neither are we reinforcing the dog's fear.

12. Is the dog nervous of the equipment?

This will usually be a case of inexperience where sympathetic handling combined with practise will solve such a problem. Instructors must however take care to ensure that the handler is not reinforcing the dog's apprehension of an obstacle by over soothing.

13. Is the dog concerned about the instructor or judge being close?

This is only likely to occur with dogs that are frightened of strangers. A good judge will usually be close to the 'A' Ramp and dog walk so therefore the instructor should get into similar positions but, if necessary, starting further away and gradually closing the distance over a period of weeks. Other people, who should preferably be strangers to the dog, should then be asked to be stooge judges so that desensitisation is carried out to strangers in general and not just the instructor.

14. Is the handler aware of the dog's sensitivities?

A dog may be sensitive to light, sound or touch. Instructors should be aware of the sensitivities of the dog under training and if the handler is unaware of them they should be advised. When a dog emerges from dark to light he may have trouble adjusting and if he is suddenly working into the sun its glare may cause him to misjudge a jump.

The dog that is sensitive to sound might not necessarily be one that is also frightened of bangs. A loud handler may need to be advised that his dog requires quiet handling. Obviously the last thing a dog sensitive to touch requires is a heavy handed handler.

If the dog under training is sensitive to touch it may be observed that his handler is too heavy handed, with direct contact and also when initial lead training is taking place.

15. Is the dog too excitable?

Whilst poor initial control can contribute to this problem usually excitability is the dog's nature but it can also be exacerbated by an excitable handler. Very often this type of dog can be seen being allowed to watch other dogs taking part in Agility and thereby becoming more wound up as he watches. Far better that he should not see others jumping, or even better still be given control exercises outside the ring, while other dogs are working, so that he learns that his handler is more important than Agility.

16. Is the dog inattentive?

There are several reasons to cause this. In the first place a dog who is nervous of people, other dogs, or noises would be liable to feel it is more important to watch out for that which he fears rather than pay attention to what he is being asked to do. If this is the case then the remedies for nervous dogs as described on pages 130-131 should be undertaken.

Dominance can also cause this problem and this will mean lowering the dogs perception of his position within the pack in domestic and exercising situations.

The dog might be bored but it is more likely that the handler does not have his respect so more work on immediate compliance with control commands should be undertaken away from the Agility area.

17. Is the dog too slow?

Perhaps the dog is generally fast but has suddenly become slow, or maybe the dog has never been fast. Some of the reasons this may occur is that the dog has been bored by over long training sessions or that he has led an inactive life prior to Agility. He may be overweight which is also not conducive to speed.

Other reasons might be that he has become what we describe as 'ring crafty' whereby he will work reasonably fast in training but knows that he need not do so in the competition ring as there is nothing the handler will do about it.

This can be a difficult problem to overcome and we would suggest that first of all in future all training should be in short sessions of just a few minutes. During these short sessions any Agility should be very much play Agility using a ball, toys or whatever will motivate the dog. In conjunction with this every effort should be made to simulate competitions during training. If possible there should be noise, applause and excitement.

Ask some of the other competition handlers to help by being part of a relay team with a baton change and run the slow dog at the end following the most excitable dog.

Sometimes using a keener dog to chase the slower one around the ring will help. Try and work it so that the faster dog starts about four or five obstacles behind the slower one.

If the dog will not play then it must be a case of back to the drawing board and try to teach him to play first of all in the house. Once he will do this progress towards outdoors and then finally using all his play incentives back on to Agility equipment.

Using food is more difficult but if the dog is definitely greedy then recalling him to the handler over a line of jumps to food held in the hand may have the effect of greater speed.

If all else fails then we would recommend a long lay off from Agility. The length of that lay off would need to be not less than three months and may be even up to a year.

GENERAL CONTROL

18. Is response to commands immediate?

We have advised that from the beginning a prospective Agility dog should have good control. One thing that is certain is that if a dog has a reasonable turn of speed then immediate reaction to commands is essential. If not elimination will be a regular occurrence when the dog takes a wrong course.

Handlers with this problem should be advised to work on their control as often as possible. No opportunity should be lost to improve response to commands.

19. When necessary does the dog turn back immediately?

Very often Agility courses will turn back by something well in excess of 90 degrees and often double that figure. If the dog under training is seen to be taking extra strides after a command then valuable time will be lost. A dog going on for 3 extra yards before turning can be wasting in excess of 3 seconds.

It may be that the handler could improve the situation by giving his turn command earlier but, in general, attention to this problem should be given. (Refer back to "Working On with Control", page 83 and "Box Training", page 112)

20. Does the dog make too wide a sweep when turning back?

A similar problem to the one above and one that can be helped by line training in a box (See page 112). It is important that the dog should turn about quickly rather than take a wide sweep for this also is a waste of ground which means wasted time. There is a saying that "time is money" but in the case of Agility "ground is time".

21. Between rounds does the dog take obstacles on his own?

Often to be seen in a class situation is a handler who completes a round, sequence, or jump only to lose their dog over another obstacle because they are now paying attention to their instructor rather than their dog. Handlers should be told that their first responsibility is to get their dog back under control before speaking to their instructor. If this means that the dog should be placed on a lead then so be it. Nothing is worse than allowing dogs to develop the habit of taking obstacles without instruction to do so. This soon becomes a habit hard to break in competition.

22. Is the dog dominant?

This is apparent when the dog is determined to be in front as the leader and therefore treats the obstacles that he should walk over as a race with his handler. Often this problem can be seen on a dog walk and is the result of either the dogs dominance instinct or a lack of earlier control.

It is likely that the dog also shows signs of dominance in domestic situations and therefore maybe the advice of a behaviourist should be sought. In the meantime the symptom can be cured by the handler holding back behind the dog who will usually slow down and wait for his handler to catch up a little. Certainly trying to race the dog to the end is not only an impossibility but just ensures the dog will leave the obstacle earlier and miss his contact.

23. Is the dog out of control?

If the dog is totally out of control on an Agility course then a complete break from Agility should be taken for between three and twelve months. During this time dog and handler should attend obedience classes and have at least one daily control session which will have nothing to do with Agility.

PRAISE.

24. Is praise being used?

Some handlers completely forget to use praise and instructors must watch out for this. Try and ensure that all dogs receive praise when applicable plus a friendly pat and word of encouragement at the end of a round.

25. Is praise being used at the wrong time?

If this happens it will elicit the wrong response from the dog who, as a result, will only become confused. There are also some beginner handlers who will literally follow an instructor's wishes by continually praising their dog, but very often at inappropriate times.

26. Is praise being given too late?

Although a handler may appear to be praising their dog at appropriate moments, are they actually praising just that little bit too late? Remember that praise must be simultaneous with a dog's actions and fractions of a second can be too late.

27. Is praise being given too early?

Similar to the above but in reverse, although a handler may appear to be praising their dog at an appropriate time are they giving that praise too early?

THE USE OF TOYS

28. Are toys being used?

Strangely enough although you might have stressed how toys and play can easily train a dog for Agility some handlers will overlook that fact. It is therefore an instructor's job to evaluate his pupils dogs and suggest toys are used where applicable.

29. Are toys being used advantageously?

Having encouraged a handler to use toys for Agility training it is now important to ensure that they are used to the best advantage. For example the timing of thrown toys is very important, as is their use as lure.

30. Is the dog toy happy?

Some dogs are so crazy for their toy that their attention is only on the toy or pocket that contains it. In such a case it is counter productive to use toys, for the dog will not be concentrating on what he should be doing.

31. Are toys suitable for all dogs?

As with the previous example of a toy happy dog, one who shows little or no interest in toys is not suitable for this type of motivation. It is an instructor who should decide whether or not using toys with any given dog is desirous.

THE USE OF TIT-BITS

32. Are tit-bits being used?

Some handlers are loathe to use food to motivate their dog when doing so might quickly teach him his handler's requirements. Instructors must decide if the dog under training would benefit from the use of food and give appropriate advice.

33. Are tit-bits being used at the correct time?

Timing when to give food to a dog is essential. Usually handlers are far too late giving tit-bits. They do not realise that their dog is now thinking about something else entirely and therefore he is rewarded for whatever the dog's current thoughts are.

Handlers who keep their food in bags or containers and only start to search for that container, let alone open it, after their dog has completed his task are giving him a false message. If food is to be used instructors must insist that it is ready between fingers and thumb before the dog commences his task. In this way it can be given to the dog at the appropriate time.

34. Is the dog besotted with tit-bits?

Obviously a dog who is so besotted with food that all his attention is on his handler and where he has concealed the tit-bits is not the right one for this kind of motivation. Far better that food is dispensed with altogether so that the handler can get his dog's attention on the task in hand.

35. Are tit-bits suitable for all dogs?

As with the example above of a food happy dog, one who shows little or no interest in food is not suitable for this type of encouragement. It is the instructor who should decide whether or not using food with any given dog is achieving the desired effect. If not then changes should be suggested.

GENERAL HANDLING MISTAKES

36. Is the voice being pitched correctly?

Many handlers get into bad habits of using a growling tone to praise their dog. This must be most confusing to a dog when the handler also uses growling tones for chastisement. It is also important to listen to a handlers general use of their voice to ensure that it is not all a boring monotone. Where necessary it should be crisp, sometimes it should be exciting, sometimes it should be firm. Ensure that your handlers are using their voices to maximum advantage. Sometimes an excitable dog is handled by someone with an excitable voice. If so vocal changes must be made.

37. Is the handler too hard?

Some people are soft by nature and others are too hard. It is this latter type that we are dealing with here. Even if the dog appears to be a tough nut, over hard handling may not be desirable for that particular dog. It is our experience that this type of handling becomes the norm because basic control has not been satisfactorily developed. A well trained dog, even one with dominant tendencies, will not need to be handled in a hard manner.

38. Is harsh handling being used?

We like to make a distinction between firm handling which, whilst not necessarily being suitable for the dog under training, is different from harsh handling which is entirely unacceptable.

Harsh handling is usually carried out in temper and it often means striking a dog or abusing him in an unacceptable manner. No matter who it is, whether a newcomer or an experienced star handler, no instructor should allow such handling. If it occurs they should be stopped immediately and at the very least be spoken to in no uncertain terms. If it is thought to be necessary other action should be taken through the club.

39. Is side changing fluent?

Changing sides is an integral part of freestyle handling but some handlers can be clumsy with it. If this is the case set up some special sequences that demand fluent changes of side. If necessary tell the handler that you will work out some sequences before next week's class and ask him to practise on them then. This is another area where planning your class is an asset to maximise use of training time.

40. Is one side favoured by the dog at some obstacles?

If so this will indicate he is still concerned about where he should be in relation to his handler rather than getting on with the job. Having noted which obstacles present such problems the instructor should set up practise sequences for handler and dog and ensure that handling is carried out on the logical side.

41. Is body positioning correct for every obstacle?

Watch handlers running sequences or complete rounds and note where they position their body at any given part of a course. Very often you will find there is room for improvement. It may be that they move too slowly into a new position or are in a totally incorrect position anyway, unwittingly giving their dog wrong information. This is made even worse when the dog hears the handler's voice or movement coming from an area which causes him to turn the wrong way. Remember in such a case ground wasted by the dog costs time. (Further information on this subject can be found on page 20)

42. Is the handler's body language tidy?

Body language has been discussed in depth on pages 19 and 20 and it is important that it is kept neat and tidy. It is yet another point to watch out for in a class.

43. Are signals and commands positive?

Instructors should watch out for poorly delivered commands and ineffective signalling. Some handlers deliver signals just with their hand and more in the manner of waving a piece of wet fish. Signals must be positive so that there is no misunderstanding by the dog.

44. Are signals and commands timed correctly?

Inexperienced handlers are likely to give commands and signals too late or too early. Even relatively experienced handlers often give their dog his instructions too late and this is a regular cause of wrong course elimination.

45. Are signals being given with the arm nearest the dog?

With odd exceptions signals should always be given by the arm nearest the dog. This is the logical one to use as the dog generally has a clear view of it. Watch out for the handler who only seems to be able to use the arm they favour. In other words the same one as their natural writing arm. This will often mean signals being given across the front of the body.

46. Does the handler take his eyes off the dog?

Perhaps the most common fault of all is when a handler takes his eyes off the dog. Sometimes they only do so momentarily but that is usually when the dog will go wrong. Even if the handler you are watching gets away with taking his eyes off the dog it should be pointed out to him for it is an easy habit to adopt. Even the most experienced handler can make this mistake so literally no one is immune from it.

47. Does the handler over handle his dog?

Some handlers constantly touch and place their dogs and this can be described as over handling. The instructor should watch carefully for such a problem and give advice accordingly.

48. Is the dog loathe to leave his handler?

It might be that the dog is nervous but far more likely is that he has never been taught to work on, or too much regimented heel work has been undertaken in the past. If necessary this dog must be taught to play and also reference to page 78 where advice on teaching working on is given will be beneficial.

49. Is the dog permanently inexperienced?

It is possible for a dog to be coming to classes intermittently for a number of years yet still not be able to get round a full course without considerable difficulty. Such a dog's handler will be dabbling at Agility and not making a definite effort to proceed further which requires practise and training. Rather than allow the dog to continue making mistakes on full courses the handler should be advised to return to sequencing and practise more frequently.

BAD HABITS

50. Is the dog barking?

First of all a dog tied up and barking is a bad enough distraction, and competition for the instructor, particularly if the class is being held indoors. The most common occurrence is a dog who, tied up, persistently barks. Some will bark from Agility excitement while others are calling their handler back. Wise is the instructor who will not allow dogs to bark in his class.

Dogs barking on the course is something else again and the first thing to realise is that it has probably been caused by the handler. For example the dog uttering just one bark or whimper as he goes over an 'A' ramp for the first time will connect any praise for negotiating the obstacle with barking although his handler will only think he is praising his attempt. If the handler is lucky, barking may only be connected to certain obstacles, if not then the dog, not stopped from this annoying habit, will eventually bark his way all round the course. It may seem funny to start with but it will always finish up as a shouting match between dog and handler.

The only certain way of avoiding this problem is to never let it happen in the first place. Whilst this is not much help to someone with this problem barking is extremely difficult to curtail. A sudden noise can be tried but there is the danger of inducing gun shyness. We have known people squirting water at their dog from a water pistol or similar, or even the instructor throwing a bucket of water over the dog. If the dog really hates water then such a remedy might work but it certainly will not work for all dogs.

One worthwhile remedy is to teach the dog to bark on command. To do so not only must the dog understand when to start but also when to stop. Subsequently the cease barking command that he will have learned can be used during Agility.

To teach a dog to bark, find anything other than Agility that motivates the dog to do so then simultaneously use the chosen speak command. Initially when teaching the dog to commence and stop barking the handler should be close to him. As progress is made a gradual movement away from the dog is desirable. Not until absolute and immediate compliance to a cease barking command has been obtained as a separate exercise should the handler be allowed to attempt to use it during Agility training or competition.

51. Is the dog circling?

I am sure that every instructor will have come across the dog that circles as he works. The lesser problem of two types of circling is the dog who turns the wrong way after jumping an obstacle prior to a turn. Once he has started to move the wrong way and subsequently discovers he is required to go in the opposite direction he will usually turn full circle to get back towards his handler. Inevitably this problem is caused by poor body language, for the fact that the handler is not using his body to convey the next direction is causing the dog to guess. More use of freestyle handling techniques and good body positioning will bring dividends. Speeding up the handlers body movement so they are fractionally earlier moving into the correct position will give the dog an earlier message and often be all that is necessary. If the dog is ahead moving to the side the dog is required to turn and giving his attention command can help.

More persistent circling can be the result of several poor initial training methods.

a) Teaching the dog to jump by continually teasing him back and forth over a hurdle with a tug or toy will soon set up a circling habit. As the dog lands he will have to turn to back jump, and this develops into a habit of jump, land and turn.

If this has caused the problem, then thrown toys over the hurdle should be used to keep the dog's interest on the toy rather than turning back to jump again. One hurdle should be used to start with, then another added until there are several that a toy can be thrown over. In other words the handler should teach his dog to work on rather than jump and turn.

Additionally practise should be carried out on courses that encourage handlers to cut corners for such courses will have few long straight lines.

b) Another cause can be a learner dog who is too fast for his handler when they start sequencing. Once the dog who has been taught to 'Work on' finds his handler is far behind he will turn to look for him. It is at this point that the dog will circle which will soon become a habit. One answer is for a faster handler to help with transitional sequencing so that the dog is not tempted to turn back. Another is to ensure that there are no long straight lines of obstacles where the dog can easily get ahead.

52. Is the handler shouting?

Unnecessary shouting is often heard. It is usually a substitute for disobedience caused by a lack of basic training. Try asking the handler to run around the course with his mouth completely shut, using just body language and signals to direct his dog. The handler might be surprised at the result and therefore you can prove that his shouting is completely unnecessary and only a case of panic or habit. If, however, shouting is necessary because the dog is barking, then an attempt should be made to stop the dog doing so (See page 139)

53. Is the dog taking his own course?

The reason for this problem is usually that Agility was commenced before proper control of the dog had been established. Another reason can be when a handler has allowed a dog to take obstacles without instructions. This may be at the end of a training round, and particularly while being spoken to by an instructor. At other times the dog may have started taking obstacles that he likes. Tunnels and tyres are often favourites, and sometimes handlers think it is great fun to watch them attempting to negotiate them without instructions. Initially it might be fun, but it must be remembered that every time the dog takes an obstacle without instructions to do so he is having a lesson in taking his own course and that is a recipe for disaster.

To start to put this problem right an instructor should advise a return to basic control work, particularly away from Agility courses. An immediately obeyed attention command should also be established so that when Agility is returned to the handler can keep the dog under control between sequence or full round attempts.

It is preferable that special sequences are devised which contain definite traps so that greater control can be used in conjunction with Agility equipment. To start with the traps must not be so difficult that the dog is constantly wrong for this would be self defeating. Far better that initially traps are reasonably easy to call the dog away from and then as the dog progresses they are made more difficult. Some box work together with tunnels after a hurdle would be an ideal exercise for most dogs to start with.

To test whether control around Agility obstacles has been established a straight line of three hurdles can be set up with no more than 5 or 6 yards or metres between. The handler should first of all be asked to send his dog over all three obstacles on three consecutive occasions. Having done that the dog should be sent again and the handler told that he should call his dog back to him before he takes the third obstacle. Until the handler can do so while remaining close to the first obstacle control cannot be said to have been established.

SPEED

54. Is the dog slow on a particular obstacle?

A dog may be just slow over a certain obstacle or obstacles and if this is the case then the dog has some apprehension connected with that obstacle. If it is just inexperience then more practise should help to quicken the dog up. If not then perhaps there is a deeper rooted problem connected with the obstacle that dates to something that has happened during initial training. Whatever might be found to be the cause it is almost certain that the only remedy will be to restore the dog's confidence. This must be done with sympathetic but positive handling with a lot of fun and play. Maybe food will be the answer for a particular dog, but certainly continuing to run the dog in what is the handler's usual fashion is unlikely to change his demeanour on that obstacle.

55. Is the dog enjoying Agility?

If the dog is not enjoying Agility then clearly something is wrong. It may be that initial incorrect teaching has caused apprehension whereby compulsion rather than play and coaxing have been the adopted training methods. The answer must lie in making Agility fun for the dog, and this can only be achieved through play training rather than something more formal.

56. Is the handler too slow?

Well sooner or later we can all suffer from slowness due to the onset of infirmity or old age. In such cases little can be done, and the handler will no doubt recognise his own limitations. However if the handler has a new young dog and it is time for sequencing there is an argument for a faster handler to teach sequencing and working on. Their is a danger that if the dog is naturally much faster than his handler he will get ahead and look back for his handler, which is one way a dog learns to start circling on the course. Once the dog understands the requirement he can be passed back to his slower handler who must now move as quickly as possible.

THE START

57. Will the dog 'Wait' at the start while his handler moves away?

This is a basic part of recall jumping first described on pages 75-77. It can be a serious problem for some who have allowed the problem to develop. The instructor should be aware of this problem which might be linked to dominance on the course. If so reference should be made to problem number 22 also more 'Wait' control training should be advised.

58. Is maximum use being made of recall jumping?

If the handler is able to leave his dog at the start an instructor should be looking to see if he is making maximum use of this ability. If he is just moving past the first hurdle and not others that are in a reasonable straight line asking why he is not doing so could be productive. It would also be interesting to note if he leaves his dog during table counting and if not why!

Handlers whose dogs will wait at the start while they move up the course should also be making use of tactical positioning for whatever reason. It may be a trap can be obscured or where the course turns the handler can make his starting position from the far side of that turn. This may have been more difficult to do if the handler had run with his dog from the start.

59. Is the handler moving off at the right time after recall jumping?

When using a recall jumping technique the handler may be moving off too slowly, not having allowed for the fact that the dog may be at top speed when he reaches him. The handler will need a few strides to get going and, unless he is doing so, he may be at a disadvantage.

60. Is the handler inadvertently teaching anticipation to start?

A clever dog will know the set-up of an Agility start and will soon learn anticipation of that start if the handler allows it to creep in. Watch for inadvertent signals transmitted by handlers who may claim their dog will not wait at the start.

61. Is the dog too close to the first hurdle?

It is good practice for an instructor to sometimes set a start very close to a first hurdle, particularly one with a single bar. 2 feet (600 mm) or less will enable you to spot those who insist on leaving their dog on the line rather than a prudent distance behind it. Of course we both would say that a start should be further than this from the first hurdle but some judges will, from ignorance, set a very tight start. Unsuspecting handlers whose dogs commence from the start line when it is close to the first hurdle, are liable to have their dogs knock down that hurdle bar or alternatively run underneath it.

62. Is the dog attaining speed before crossing the start line?

If the handler starts his dog on the start line rather than just before it he has less chance of his dog attaining good speed before passing the start. It may only make one or two hundredths of a second difference but final places tend to change hands for such small amounts of time.

63. Is the dog too far away from the first hurdle?

Some handlers may wish to take starting their dog far from the first hurdle to the extreme. In fact we have known a handler who would think nothing of starting 20 yards outside the ring. Clearly this is taking starting speed to ridiculous lengths and an instructor should discourage it.

64. Is the dog over the start line?

A handler who leaves his dog on the start line is in danger of the dog actually being beyond it. When starting the handler needs all his concentration on the dog rather than to be told by the starter to move his dog back. Of course with electronic timing the clock would have started anyway.

65. Is the dog flattening over the first jump(s)?

Often this is a problem associated with recall jumping. However it is the authors' considered opinion that it can be due to wrongly taught initial hurdle training. If a handlers dog is flattening then it should be pointed out and discussed.

HURDLE TYPE OBSTACLES

66. Is the dog knocking down lightweight poles?

This is a common mistake and one that can be traced back to the use of such poles during training. Some dogs will think nothing of knocking into lightweight poles with their legs and it can become a habit. The answer is for heavier weight poles to be used and indeed we recommend that all training should be carried out with wooden poles of at least an 1.5" (38 mm) diameter. This ensures sufficient weight to encourage dogs not to touch them without being dangerous.

67. Is the dog taking off too late?

Some dogs, particularly those who are inexperienced, will take off too late. Once again apprehension of hurdles may have caused the problem or more practise may be the answer. The instructor must decide why and if it is inexperience then the answer is more practise particularly with hurdle only sequences. If it is decided that it is apprehension then reteaching hurdle jumping with a lot of play should rectify the dog's dilemma.

68. Is the dog taking off too soon?

We generally refer to this problem as 'Standing off'. Again it can be purely inexperience and therefore maybe the dog has been progressed too fast. If this is so we would suggest that the dog is taken back to some straight forward hurdle sequences and then to sequences that include other obstacles as well as at least one hurdle. As a general rule it may also be beneficial to lower the hurdle height.

Another reason can be that the dog is instantly obeying his handler's jumping command which is being delivered too soon. To test this theory tell the handler not to give any command but to run towards a hurdle and see if the dog will jump in his own time. Obviously if this is found to be the problem it will be far better if for some time the dog is not given a command to jump relying instead on signals and body language. If necessary signals must also be suspended for a while.

69. Is the dog running under single hurdle poles?

This is almost certainly the result of poor early training. If single pole hurdles had been used from the start, rather than rushing to increase height to stop the dog's tendency to run underneath by placing more bars on the hurdle, the problem would not have arisen in the first place. The remedy must be back to the beginning and to lower a single pole to the point where the dog will not try to run underneath. It should then be gradually raised, and any time the dog tries to run under it the height must be lowered to that which was previously successful. Of course the dog's fitness should also be considered.

70. Is the dog flattening?

This describes the dog who jumps with a low trajectory. We believe this to be caused by inappropriate initial hurdle training for the dog has not learned the right trajectory. It can be caused by moving on to sequences too quickly and concentrating on speed. By doing so the dog is placing too much prominence on taking each obstacle before he has learned the best way to do so.

Usually dogs that flatten are much more likely to do so when recall jumping towards their handler and it is the extra speed that causes the problem. Such a dog is usually also quite happy to knock down lightweight poles.

To remedy this dog's habit, first of all heavier weight poles should be used and in training he should be trained on hurdles that are one or two inches (25/50 mm) over maximum height.

71. Is the dog a lazy jumper?

A dog who has a good jumping trajectory yet judges the height of the jump so critically that he knocks down poles can be described as being a lazy jumper. This can often be a problem with an overweight dog but it also applies to dogs who never expend more energy than necessary. Inevitably such a dog will have had much practise in knowing just how high the maximum height is. To counter the problem, jump heights should be varied between 2 inches (50 mm) below and above maximum jumping height.

If lightweight plastic poles are being used heavier weight poles should also be used, and the reintroduction of toys thrown while jumping may change the dog's action. Be careful not to confuse this type with the fast dog who flattens his trajectory.

72. Is the dog banking wells and walls?

Banking is a term derived from the horse world to described a dog that uses his paws to gain purchase on an obstacle that he should clear. It is usually caused by inexperience on the dog's part or teaching the obstacle too soon, and definitely before the dog has mastered full jumping height technique over ordinary hurdles.

Banking can also be caused by a dog that is standing off before jumping. If that is thought to be the cause see page 145 for advice on this problem.

We would suggest that you should first determine whether banking is a definite habit or just the result of inexperience. If it is the latter then the answer will be obvious. However we will view it here as a persistent problem.

Try and make surfaces that the dog is using to gain purchase unstable. Dogs dislike something moving beneath their feet and by making the top unstable many dogs will prefer to clear the obstacle rather than to try and gain purchase half way across.

Another help can be to place a hurdle in front of the obstacle so that the dog views it as one to be cleared. In this way some dogs will learn that the technique required is the same as a hurdle.

73. Is the dog measuring his jumps?

We use this term to describe the dog who hesitates just before a jump type obstacle in an effort to gauge the best possible time to jump. Usually his jumping action will not be fluent and from our experience it shows that there is something wrong. It may be that the dog is too old and becoming stiff or he may be carrying an injury. Certainly, if unsure, veterinary advice should be sought before jumping is continued.

TABLE.

74. Could the dog be faster onto the table?

Some dogs approach to a table is to slow down or get too get too close before jumping up on it. Usually it is a result of poor initial training. Obviously basic training should be returned to in an effort to teach the dog to change his approach habit. This should be carried out with more fun and games for we would suggest that initial lessons may have included apprehension which resulted in such a jumping action.

75. Is the dog quick into the down?

There are brilliant dogs who are almost in a down position before they touch the table. These are of course few and far between. As usual the problem with a dog that is slow into the down can be traced back to teaching Agility table training before the dog had learned to be quick into a down on the ground. If a handler really wants to improve the speed of his dogs down then it is back to control training and until it has been perfected on the ground faster results cannot be expected on an Agility table.

76. Is more than one 'Down' command necessary?

Continuing to push the dog down on to the table in training is a very slow and ineffectual way of correcting this problem. Again reverting to the beginning and training for an immediate response to a single command on the ground will be appropriate. Until that has been accomplished it would be better that tables are not practised so that the dog is not reminded of his bad habits.

77. Can the dog be left in a 'Wait'?

Quite often it will be found that a dog that cannot be left at the start cannot be left at the table. A handler that has to stand over his dog during the table count is actually telling everybody that he does not have complete control over his dog. Again it is a fault that goes back to initial training whereby a handler has been allowed to commence Agility before basic control has been established. In this case the 'Wait'.

To put matters right 'Wait' training should be practised under a variety of conditions as something apart from Agility and the table. Leaving the dog in a down on the ground for half a yard (450 mm) to start with then gradually increasing distance until 10 or 20 yards or metres can be achieved without problem is how to build up distance.

Body language must not transmit wrong messages thus encouraging the dog to move. Until able to run away from the dog without him moving or becoming agitated, no attempt should be made to revert to table work in Agility.

When the basic problem has been cured then a table can be reintroduced, but as a single obstacle rather than part of a course. All exercises practised with a dog in the 'Wait' position on the ground must now be practised on a table before it is included as part of a sequence or complete round.

78. Is the dog being retaught that his handler will stand close?

A dog that has been taught a reliable 'Wait' which can easily be used at the table can soon inadvertently be taught that his handler will always stand close beside him at a table. This can come about by a handler not wishing to risk moving away from it during competition and often during training as well.

An additional reason an initial good 'Wait' is breaking down is that possibly the exercise is no longer practised during ordinary domestic circumstances. The dog soon learns the Agility exercise means the handler will be with him and when he does try to move away the dog moves as well. Instructors should watch for this during training insisting that handlers whose dog will wait make a point of moving away. Those who will not wait must go back to initial control training as an exercise that has nothing to do with Agility.

79. Is the dog going under or to the sides of the table?

A dog that runs under the table is usually inexperienced. It may be that initial teaching has been to place an obstruction, such as a board, at the table so the dog cannot run underneath. There is nothing wrong with this for the first few successful attempts, but if allowed to continue it has the same effect as teaching dogs hurdles with more than one pole. In other words the dog does not learn to jump on the table without a barrier beneath

Whilst most judges allow the dog to get on to the table from three sides but not the back edge it is not good practise to allow it to happen. Obviously it wastes time. It can be caused by poor initial training where the habit has been allowed to develop. Also it might be as a result of poor body language which has given the dog wrong information and only at the last moment does he realise that the table is next. Body language and positioning can soon be pointed out by the instructor, but for all other reasons listed above it is back to some basic work on the table alone and then as part of a sequence.

80. Is use being made of handler repositioning during the count?

While a handler may have the ability to make his dog wait an instructor should watch carefully to ensure that maximum use is being made by the handler to get into the best position for the next sequence of obstacles. Very often there will be an opportunity for the handler to either save running a few paces by moving up the course and/or taking up the next position. Such an opportunity may involve a change of sides or using body position to advantage.

81. Is the dog anticipating the command 'Go'?

Some handlers are so anxious to get on that as soon as a judge says 'Go' they are off with their dog. Sometimes it is simultaneous with the command 'Go'. There is nothing wrong with this until the dog starts to anticipate the command in competition and then a judge is entitled to impose a penalty. Instructors should be aware of this possibility and therefore during training it can be very good practise for 'Go' to be called several times while the handler makes no attempt to move the dog on. After the last 'Go' there should then be a slight pause before the dog is moved and in this way anticipation is avoided or overcome.

TUNNELS

82. Is the dog slow through tunnels?

Most dogs love a tunnel and those that do are generally quick through them. Not all are completely happy with the collapsible tunnel and some dislike heavy material such as plastic, while others dislike a wet tunnel. For whatever reason a dog may not be as quick through the tunnel as he could be and an instructor should be aware that more speed through should be possible. This can be achieved by play and a thrown toy, or ball as the dog exits is ideal for this purpose. A greedy dog may speed up for food which he must learn would be placed at least 3 yards in a straight line from the exit.

83. Does the dog come to a stop inside tunnels?

Occasionally a learner dog can become quite awkward and decide that once in a tunnel he is not going to come out. Usually the flexible pipe tunnel is chosen for such inaction although there are dogs who will go into the collapsible tunnel entrance but will not go through the material. In such cases the instructor should advise that a return to basic training should be made with more work on a closed up tunnel while the dog is on the lead.

84. Is the dog tunnel happy?

An instructor must be very careful to watch out for the tunnel happy dog. Some dogs can become almost addicted to tunnels and their habit is that they cannot get enough of them. If this is to become a problem it can be spotted very early on and such dogs handlers must be made aware of the dangers. At first when he starts rushing through tunnels of his own accord they will think it funny and then after several eliminations fun becomes frustration.

It is one of those problems that has no real cure and therefore that old fashioned remedy of never let it happen in the first place is the answer. If one of your handlers has this problem then the golden rule must be that as soon as a sequence or round is finished then the dog should go back on lead before he has a chance to feed his addiction.

Control training with a single tunnel is the only thing that will contain the problem.

85. Is the collapsible tunnel straight?

Just as it is the judge's responsibility to ensure that the collapsible tunnel is straight so it is an instructor's responsibility at class. Whilst a judge usually deputes someone to ensure it is straightened for each dog so can the instructor. The whole point is that a dog should never be allowed to become unnecessarily entangled in a tunnel.

86. Is the collapsible tunnel interior wet?

It may be that you are lucky in that obstacles can be left out from one week to another. Whilst training day may appear fine a previous days wet may have left a great puddle of water inside a plastic collapsible tunnel. A dog can get quite a surprise when he rushes through the tunnel and comes out soaking so, in such circumstances, it is an instructor's job to check before initial use is made of the tunnel.

87. Is the dog used to heavy, lightweight, dark and light tunnels?

If the tunnel that you normally use for training is made of lightweight material that allows much light through, then it is important that your handlers are counselled to practise on tunnels that have darker and heavier material. If not the dogs may well refuse such a tunnel in competition.

HOOP OR TYRE

88. Is the dog jumping through the tyre frame?

This problem can be attributed to inexperience or where the dog only occasionally makes this mistake. In most cases the handler probably progressed too quickly on this obstacle before his dog really understood how to negotiate it. Every time a dog attempts a tyre then he has a lesson about using it. It is therefore important that he does not learn the wrong lesson, such as frame jumping, for if it happens often enough he may occasionally revert to this wrong passage through.

Once again reversion to a lot of work with a tyre is called for. Initially the handler should be close to that tyre and then he should gradually move further away and use sequences containing a tyre. The dog should never be allowed to make this mistake again during training. Practising in a similar manor on other equipment at other venues will also pay dividends.

89. Is the dog running under the tyre?

This is a similar problem to the above but almost certainly a case of the tyre being raised too quickly for an inexperienced dog. More basic work on an initially lowered tyre is the answer so that the habit of running under is lost.

90. Does the dog mistime his jump and hit the tyre?

Inexperienced dogs can be prone to mistiming their jump and therefore hit the tyre as they try and jump through. It may be that they go through but are knocked off line as they do so. This is another case where the instructor should advise that more preliminary work should be done on a tyre, for obviously the dog does not have sufficient experience with this obstacle.

91. Does the handler take his eyes off the dog at the tyre?

A common mistake is for a handler to take his eyes off the dog at any time, but at a tyre it is quite surprising how many handlers are unaware that their dog has made a mistake. This lack of knowledge must imply that they took their eyes off the dog and indeed the instructor will be able to see it happen. Advice should be given that they should be in a position to ensure the dog has correctly jumped the tyre.

92. Is a positive signal given to avoid mistakes?

In an earlier chapter we discussed how signals should be given. Even though handlers may have learned to positively signal during early instruction bad habits can soon creep in, and the handler needs to be made aware that they may not be conveying instructions concisely to the dog, and particularly at this obstacle.

LONG JUMP

93. Is the dog making a wrong entry or exit?

From the beginning dogs should always be taught a straight approach to a long jump and then this problem will not arise. Invariably it is as a result of progressing too soon on sequences that do not have a straight approach. Once again the dog will soon learn the wrong habit and, on odd occasions, he will revert to former incorrect learning.

94. Is the dog knocking down long jump units?

If a dog is regularly knocking down long jump units inevitably it will be a fault of initial training. Going back to first long jump lessons will help but the fault may be able to be cured by placing a hurdle pole in the middle of the jump. It should be that little bit higher than the tallest long jump unit and its aim will be to encourage the dog to make more height. If sufficient practise is undertaken then that dog's habitual trajectory can be changed.

95. Is the dog walking on the long jump units?

A dog walking on the units has not been taught thoroughly. The remedy is to start at the beginning teaching the dog to jump over one unit and then gradually progressing. It is the authors belief that, whilst it is common for five units to make up a long jump at a maximum of 5 feet (15 cm), inexperienced dogs are encouraged to walk over them as five units mean they will be close together. For training it should be four maximum and for the dog with a problem even less and this will be determined by his size.

96. Is the dog walking through units?

Dogs that walk through long jump units, that is they touch the ground between each one, are doing so because they have been asked to jump too long too quickly. It therefore appears to be easier for them to walk between the units. Instructors should take the dog and handler back to the beginning on one unit only, then carefully supervise addition of a second unit when the time is right.

CONTACT EQUIPMENT

97. Is any method being used?

It is easy to see when handlers are using what we call hit and hope routines for contacts and are therefore not really employing a method. If an instructor suspects this then he should ask his pupil what method they are employing. It may be that they think they have a method but are not using it correctly.

98. Is the dog missing the up contact?

A dog that misses the up contact on any contact obstacle is usually one of the larger breeds or one that is inexperienced. Sometimes just more experience will correct the problem, or the dog may require assistance. One way is for the dog to be taught a momentary down right up close to the obstacle but we have never been entirely happy with such a method. The other which we favour is for hoops to be used (see page 69). A hoop in front of the up side contact will teach the dog a habit of ascending an obstacle that, once learned, will guarantee that the dog always makes the up contact. That is if sufficient hoop and contact work are practised.

99. Is the dog jumping off too soon?

A dog that is jumping off before touching the down contact is having a habit lesson at doing so each time it happens. An instructor's first task should be to stop the habit developing any further, and this may mean asking the handler to stop using that particular obstacle until a definite method has been decided upon. Using hoops (see pages 69-70) in conjunction with establishing a method will be the answer.

100. Does a command to stop on mean jump off?

Some handlers develop a method that they think keeps their dog on the contact but in effect the dog jumps off after a certain set pattern of commands. For instance on a dog walk as the dog starts to descend the handler may say to his dog 'You wait, you wait, you wait, you wait' The dog will be slowly descending while the handler uses these words and usually by the last command he will either just be making contact or fractionally missing it. The dog, having learned the rhythm of these four commands, knows that he jumps off after the fourth command. Sometimes he will just make the contact and on other occasions he will not. It may be any form of words that are used and they can be accompanied by a signal but the effect is the same.

In cases such as these either a whole new method should be employed (see chapter 4) or at the very least this problem should be pointed out to the handler so that the dog's rhythmic understanding becomes confused and he no longer anticipates leaving.

101. Is handler movement telling the dog to leave prematurely?

Instructors should watch carefully for the slightest body movement that prematurely tells a dog to move off the obstacle. Some dogs, particularly Collies, will pick up on fractional movements so handlers must be taught to be vigilant.

102. Is the handler crowding the dog at the contact?

A common fault is for a handler to crowd his dog on the obstacle either in front of him or by leaning just slightly over the contact. This can cause the dog to mildly panic and therefore to jump off.

103. Is body movement making the dog move off to the side?

Similar to the previous problem a dog may see an arm or body movement as a threat and therefore, to avoid it, get off the obstacle on the opposite side to the handler. It may be that his handler has been trying to hold the dog on the contact and he resents this, hence his haste to avoid the arm.

104. Is the contact method being properly applied?

A handler may be using one of the methods that you have recommended and telling you that it doesn't work. Whilst they may not have consistently applied the method another might be that they have not applied that method properly. If so persuade them that they have not got it right and go through the method again with them.

105. If used is the dog missing out the hoops?

If hoops are being used during training and the dog is bye passing or jumping over them, then clearly either that dog has not had sufficient hoop training or insufficient care has been taken with initial use of hoop and obstacle.

106. Does the contact method need changing?

If a handler is not succeeding with the method employed, and providing it is being applied properly, then maybe you should advise a change of method. It might be that they have successfully used a method for some time but the dog has become wise to it and his keenness to anticipate is overriding the boring consistency of his handler's method. It is not unusual for method that has previously been successful to no longer be effective.

107. Is the dog being slowed or stopped too far up the down side?

Some handlers using a method that requires the dog to be slowed, in their panic to stop their dog jumping off the contact, slow him too soon. This means that he stops far too high up the down side and now his routine of being brought slowly down wastes valuable time. After a while the dog will stop too high by habit almost judging this point to a fraction.

108. Is the handler trying to grab the dog?

We very much dislike a rough method of handling whereby handlers attempt to grab their dog by the scruff of the neck in an effort to stop premature departure. This can cause resentment by the dog and soon he may employ an avoidance technique such as prematurely jumping off to avoid being grabbed.

109. Is the dog racing the handler?

Some dogs will perceive contact obstacles as a race, in fact they usually want to be up front throughout the round. This is the dominant type of dog and, apart from adopting methods of reducing dominance during domestic life, it will be wise for the handler to opt out of the race. This is done by the handler hanging back well behind which in itself often causes the dog to slow down.

110. Is the dog nervous over the equipment?

Should the dog be displaying any signs of worry about a contact obstacle then his handler should revert to play or food training in an effort to give the dog confidence. Needless to say this should be done practising on the particular obstacle and until overcome complete rounds should not be reintroduced.

111. Does the dog have sufficient speed over the obstacle?

Other than supreme fitness and being able to try and out run the dog one of the best ways to gain more speed over a contact obstacle is to use play training. There is always a danger that play will allow the dog to miss contacts, therefore we advise this play training to be used in conjunction with hoops. (see chapter 4)

WEAVING POLES

112. Is the dog making entry mistakes.

A classic case of inexperience is the most likely reason but not the only one. Even an experienced dog mid way through his Agility career can start to make mistakes upon entry and therefore counter measures should be suggested. For example before reverting to basic weave training the instructor can suggest that only a very straight approach from several yards or metres away should be used. As the dog regains confidence then more angled approaches should be gradually tried.

113. Is the dog making mistakes after correct entry?

Of course this can be inexperience for the dog needs to develop his rhythm. Handlers should always be advised to restart the dog rather than to correct them in the middle and to be aware that where the mistake is being made they should give the dog greater vocal, signal, and if necessary, body language assistance. If the problem persists then it should be back to initial weave training, maybe by using a better system such as the confined channel method.

114. Is the dog missing out one or more poles at the end?

A dog missing out one or more poles at the end may be anticipating the next obstacle or, more likely, his basic training has not included 12 and 13 weaving poles. With such a dog it would be better for the handler to revert to their initial pole training using greater numbers of poles than before.

115. Are odd and even numbers of weave poles being trained for?

This is similar to the above but might involve a lesser number of poles. A dog only trained on either an odd or even number of poles can become confused because odd numbers mean that he will exit to the right and even numbers mean that he will exit to the left. When he is asked to exit in a way that he is unused to he will become confused. The solution is to have the handler initially practise with either odd or even numbers of weaving poles so that the exit side that is giving the problem has maximum practise.

116. Is the handler setting up the dog to his best advantage?

A handler may not be using body positioning to the best advantage, therefore the dog is approaching the poles at an angle he is unused to and mistakes at entry are occurring.

117. Should the handler be ahead of his dog at the weave?

It may be that more speed can be obtained through the poles by the handler getting ahead of his dog and encouraging him. This is worth an experiment with a dog that might be able to move through the poles faster. The instructor must however bear in mind that initial training that should have allowed for the dog to weave irrespective of his handler's position is not destroyed by this remedy.

118. Should the handler be behind his dog at the weave?

Some dogs can feel pressured and reluctant with their handler right beside them. If this is the case then it is worth asking the handler to experiment with urging his dog on from a position about a yard or metre behind.

119. Is the handler too close?

Similar to the above the handler may be getting too close to his dog. If this is a regular occurrence then obviously training so that the dog will weave irrespective of his handlers position has been abandoned and the instructor should enquire why.

120. Is the dog being retaught that his handler will be beside him?

Usually this problem occurs because the handler wants to play it safe, not only in competition but also when training complete rounds. If the handler runs alongside his dog often enough then he will be retaught that this is where his handler should be. If the handler now asks the dog to weave when he is not beside him then the dog will become confused and make mistakes.

121. Can the handler work the dog from either side of the weave?

If the handler consistently chooses to handle his dog on one side which will usually be the left, even though the course suggests that the opposite side to usual is employed, the handler should be encouraged to reteach his dog that he should weave irrespective of the side his handler chooses to be on. (See page 49 to 57 on Weaving)

122. Is the dog becoming weave happy.

Just as some dogs can become tunnel happy or tyre happy so can a dog become weave happy. This kind of dog will take any opportunity to weave. If the dog can be sent forward to weave, when training on this obstacle only, and the handler does not move his body to one side and call the dog to him he will return by weaving. This is generally how the problem starts, so instructors must be certain that when the dog has weaved the handler has moved away to call the dog who should be placed on a lead unless absolute attention is to be paid to him.

A golden rule for all training is never to allow a handler's dog to take any obstacle unless he has been given instructions to do so. This applies very much to weaving poles.

123. Are the poles regularly spaced to produce a weave rhythm.

All weaving poles, particularly those that are secured by being pressed into the ground, should be evenly spaced. We believe that regular spacing of a normal width allows the dog to obtain a rhythm. We are very much against judges who are tempted to use gimmicks such as spacing the poles at different intervals. This is only an attempt to trap or slow the dogs down.

124. Does the weave command need improvement or adjustment?

Instructors should be aware of the weave command being used. Some handlers will give the command once while others find it necessary to repeat it more than once. Some like to use a continuous sound or clap their dogs through with encouragement. None of these systems are wrong but tones of voice may need adjusting or else the instructor may wish to experiment with a continuous sound.

Summary:-

Fitness and safety

1. Is the dog's movement sound?
2. Is the dog overweight?
3. Is the dog too young or too old?
4. Is the handler fit?
5. Is the right footwear being worn?
6. Is the equipment safe?
7. Is the course ready for the dog?

The dog

8. Is the dog the right material for Agility?
9. Is the dog nervous of strangers?
10. Is the dog nervous of other dogs?
11. Is the dog nervous of thunder and bangs?
12. Is the dog nervous of the equipment?
13. Is the dog concerned about the instructor or judge being close?
14. Is the handler aware of the dog's sensitivities?
15. Is the dog too excitable?
16. Is the dog inattentive?
17. Is the dog too slow?

General control

18. Is response to commands immediate?
19. When necessary does the dog turn back immediately?
20. Does the dog make too wide a sweep when turning back?
21. Between rounds does the dog take obstacles on his own?
22. Is the dog dominant?
23. Is the dog out of control?

Praise

24. Is praise being used?
25. Is praise being used at the wrong time?
26. Is praise being given too late?
27. Is praise being given too early?

The use of toys

28. Are toys being used?
29. Are toys being used advantageously?
30. Is the dog toy happy?
31. Are toys suitable for all dogs?

The use of tit-bits
   32. Are tit-bits being used?
   33. Are tit-bits being used at the correct time?
   34. Is the dog besotted with tit-bits?
   35. Are tit-bits suitable for all dogs?

General handling mistakes
   36. Is the voice being pitched correctly?
   37. Is the handler too hard?
   38. Is harsh handling being used?
   39. Is side changing fluent?
   40. Is one side favoured by the dog at some obstacles?
   41. Is body positioning correct for every obstacle?
   42. Is the handler's body language tidy?
   43. Are signals and commands positive?
   44. Are signals and commands timed correctly?
   45 Are signals being given with the arm nearest the dog?
   46. Does the handler take his eyes off the dog?
   47. Does the handler over handle his dog?
   48. Is the dog loathe to leave his handler?
   49. Is the dog permanently inexperienced?

Bad habits
   50. Is the dog barking?
   51. Is the dog circling?
   52. Is the handler shouting?
   53. Is the dog taking his own course?

Speed
   54. Is the dog slow on a particular obstacle?
   55. Is the dog enjoying Agility?
   56. Is the handler too slow?

The start
   57. Will the dog 'Wait' at the start while his handler moves away?
   58. Is maximum use being made of recall jumping?
   59. Is the handler moving off at the right time after recall jumping?
   60. Is the handler inadvertently teaching anticipation to start?
   61. Is the dog too close to the first hurdle?
   62. Is the dog attaining speed before crossing the start line?
   63. Is the dog too far away from the first hurdle?
   64. Is the dog over the start line?
   65. Is the dog flattening over the first jump(s)?

Hurdle type obstacles

66. Is the dog knocking down lightweight poles?
67. Is the dog taking off too late?
68. Is the dog taking off too soon?
69. Is the dog running under single hurdle poles?
70. Is the dog flattening?
71. Is the dog a lazy jumper?
72. Is the dog banking wells and walls?
73. Is the dog measuring his jumps?

Table

74. Could the dog be faster onto the table?
75. Is the dog quick into the down?
76. Is more than one 'Down' command necessary?
77. Can the dog be left in a 'Wait'?
78. Is the dog being retaught that his handler will stand close?
79. Is the dog going under or to the sides of the table?
80. Is use being made of handler repositioning during the count?
81. Is the dog anticipating the command 'Go'?

Tunnels

82. Is the dog slow through tunnels?
83. Does the dog come to a stop inside tunnels?
84. Is the dog tunnel happy?
85. Is the collapsible tunnel straight?
86. Is the collapsible tunnel interior wet?
87. Is the dog used to heavy, lightweight, dark and light tunnels?

Hoop (Tyre)

88. Is the dog jumping through the tyre frame?
89. Is the dog running under the tyre?
90. Does the dog mistime his jump and hit the tyre?
91. Does the handler take his eyes off the dog at the tyre?
92. Is a positive signal given to avoid mistakes?

Long jump

93. Is the dog making a wrong entry or exit?
94. Is the dog knocking down long jump units?
95. Is the dog walking on the long jump units?
96. Is the dog walking through units?

Contact equipment

97. Is any method being used?
98. Is the dog missing the up contact?
99. Is the dog jumping off too soon?
100. Does a command to stop on mean jump off?
101. Is handler movement telling the dog to leave prematurely?
102. Is the handler crowding the dog at the contact?
103. Is body movement making the dog move off to the side?
104. Is the contact method being properly applied?
105. If used is the dog missing out the hoops?
106. Does the contact method need changing?
107. Is the dog being slowed or stopped too far up the down side?
108. Is the handler trying to grab the dog?
109. Is the dog racing the handler?
110. Is the dog nervous over the equipment?
111. Does the dog have sufficient speed over the obstacle?

Weaving poles

112. Is the dog making entry mistakes?
113. Is the dog making mistakes after correct entry?
114. Is the dog missing out one or more poles at the end?
115. Are odd and even numbers of weave poles being trained for?
116. Is the handler setting up the dog to his best advantage?
117. Should the handler be ahead of his dog at the weave?
118. Should the handler be behind his dog at the weave?
119. Is the handler too close?
120. Is the dog being retaught that his handler will be beside him?
121. Can the handler work the dog from either side of the weave?
122. Is the dog becoming weave happy?
123. Are the poles regularly spaced to produce a weave rhythm?
124. Does the weave command need improvement or adjustment?